MASTERS OF ART

CHAGALL

GIANNI POZZI

◆

ILLUSTRATED BY
CLAUDIA SARACENI, L.R. GALANTE

PETER BEDRICK BOOKS
NEW YORK

♦ HOW THE INFORMATION IS PRESENTED

...sello
...research:
...nerine Forden
Graphic design:
Oliviero Ciriaci
Art direction:
Laura Ottina Davis
Sebastiano Ranchetti
Page design:
Laura Ottina Davis
Editorial:
Andrea Bachini
Renzo Rossi
English translation:
Brett Shapiro
Editor, English-language edition:
Ruth Nason

© 1997 DoGi s.r.l.
Florence, Italy

English language text © 1997 by
DoGi s.r.l. /Peter Bedrick Books

Published by
PETER BEDRICK BOOKS
2112 Broadway
New York NY 10023

Library of Congress
Cataloging-in-Publication Data
Pozzi, Gianni.
[Chagall. English]
Chagall / Gianni Pozzi ; illustrations by
Claudia Saraceni, L.R. Galante.
p. cm. – (Masters of art)
includes index.
ISBN 0-87226-527-7
1. Chagall, Marc 1887–1985. 2. Artists –
Russia (Federation) – Biography.
I. Saraceni, Claudia. II. Galante, L. R.
III. Title. IV Series: Masters of art
(Peter Bedrick Books)
N6999.C46P6813 1997
709'.2–dc21 [B] 97–7330 CIP AC

Printed by Amilcare Pizzi,
Cinisello Balsamo (Milan)
Photolitho: Venanzoni DTP, Florence
First edition 1997

Every double-page spread is a chapter in its own right, devoted to an aspect of the life and art of Marc Chagall or the major artistic and cultural developments of his time. The text at the top of the left-hand page (1) and the large central illustration are concerned with this main theme. The text in italics (2) gives a chronological account of events in Chagall's life. The other material (photographs, paintings, and drawings) enlarges on the central theme.

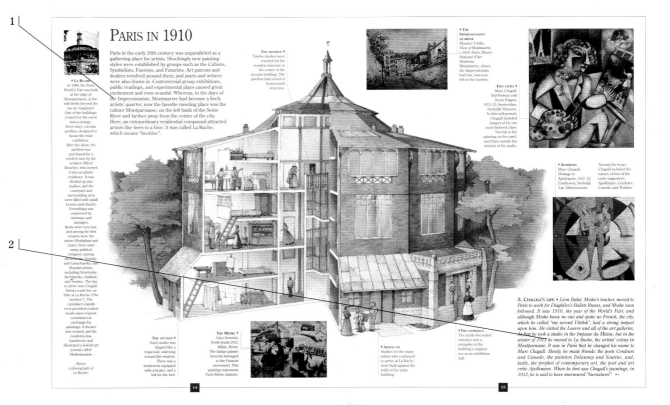

Some pages focus on major works by Marc Chagall. They include the following information: an account of the painting's history (1); a description of the content and imagery of the work (2); a critical analysis and detailed examination of its formal aspects (3). There are also reproductions of works by other artists, to set Chagall's work in its historical context and demonstrate its uniqueness.

CONTENTS

CONTEMPORARIES

The life of the Russian-born artist Marc Chagall spanned almost a hundred years (1887 to 1985), during which time the world around him underwent many profound changes. He witnessed and, in some cases, was closely involved in the great events of the 20th century, and he contributed to the development of new ways of thinking about art. However, although he associated with such painters as Picasso, Malevich, and Soutine, and such poets as Apollinaire and Cendrars, Chagall remained faithful to his earliest inspiration. His Russian Jewish (particularly Hasidic) background provided him with a wealth of stimuli and references. His paintings show an extraordinary ability to combine the traditional and the modern.

✦ **TEACHER**
Yehuda Pen was Chagall's first painting teacher in Vitebsk. After the Russian Revolution, he taught at the Vitebsk Academy where Chagall was director.

✦ **CHAGALL'S PARENTS**
His father Zakhar and his mother Feiga-Ita. In many paintings, Chagall portrayed his father as big, stooping and sad, and his mother as petite and lively.

LENIN ✦
(1870-1924)
The 20th century's most famous revolutionary who became the leader of the new Soviet Union. He met Chagall in Paris in 1910.

IDA CHAGALL ✦
(1916-1994)
Daughter of Chagall and Bella. After her father's death, she created a foundation for the study and preservation of his work.

✦ **BELLA ROSENFELD**
(1895-1944)
Chagall's first wife. She is portrayed in many of his paintings, from 1909, when the couple met, until long after her death.

✦ **KAZIMIR MALEVICH**
(1878-1935)
A famous Russian painter, both friend and enemy of Chagall, and, with him, a central figure in the creation of the Academy in Vitebsk.

✦ **SERGEI DIAGHILEV**
(1872-1929)
This extraordinary impresario made Russian ballet and painting known world-wide.

✦ **LEV ROSENBERG,**
KNOWN AS LÉON BAKST
(1866-1924)
One of Chagall's teachers in St. Petersburg, he became set designer for the Ballets Russes in Paris.

MARC CHAGALL ♦
(1887-1985)
His real name was Moshe Zakharovich Shagal. After he moved to Paris in 1910, he changed Moshe Shagal into the French Marc Chagall and eliminated the patronymic.

ANATOLI ♦ LUNACHARSKY
(1875-1933)
Appointed by Lenin as People's Commissar for Education, in 1918 he charged Chagall with founding an art academy in Vitebsk.

♦ POETS
The poets Blaise Cendrars (1887-1961) and Guillaume Apollinaire (1880-1918) were among the first to appreciate the works of the young, unknown artist Chagall after he arrived in Paris in 1910.

ART DEALERS ♦
The great French art dealer Ambroise Vollard (1865-1939) and his German colleague Herwarth Walden were impressed by Chagall's painting and helped to promote his work.

♦ ROBERT DELAUNAY
Robert Delaunay (1885-1941) and his wife, Sonia Terk (1885-1979), were very close to Marc and Bella Chagall, especially in Paris in 1923-30.

♦ CHAIM SOUTINE
(1894-1943)
A Russian painter and a great friend of Chagall. They both had studios at La Ruche, in Paris.

♦ ANDRÉ MALRAUX
(1901-1976)
A French writer and friend of Chagall. As Minister of Cultural Affairs in the 1960s, he supported the creation of the Nice Museum.

♦ VALENTINA BRODSKY
(1905-1993)
Chagall's second wife, whom he called Vava,

helped create the Museum of the Biblical Message in Nice, France.

VITEBSK

At the end of the 19th century, in spite of its port on the Dvina River, its blossoming industry, and the railroad line connecting it to St. Petersburg and Kiev, the small city of Vitebsk still retained the aspect of a large country village, with its narrow streets, old low houses, courtyards, and gardens. However, it did have some imposing Orthodox Christian churches and many beautiful synagogues. The Jewish community, comprising almost one half of Vitebsk's 50,000 inhabitants, had a reasonable existence, helped by its close network of relatives and neighbors. There was less prejudice and discrimination against Jews in Vitebsk than in most of Tsarist Russia. Before becoming part of the Russian empire, Vitebsk had long been dominated first by Lithuania and then by Poland, and the memory of this earlier history lingered on in the city's character. It was a frontier city where different cultures and religions coexisted.

♦ HASIDISM

Hasidism (the term derives from the Hebrew *hasid*, meaning pious) is a religious movement within Judaism that began in Poland in the early 18th century and spread widely throughout Eastern Europe – Russia, Poland, Romania, and Hungary.
While orthodox Judaism emphasized learning and knowledge of the scriptures, Hasidism stressed personal experience of God's presence in all of creation and in every aspect of daily life. This experience was open to all with pious hearts, rather than only to the learned.
According to Hasidism, the observance of religious rules and forms was less important than the inner feeling that allowed the pious to commune with God. This inner feeling expressed itself as joy, and therefore whatever caused joy had a religious value.
Unlike orthodox Judaism, Hasidism allowed the artistic portrayal of the human body and was rich in legends and magical tales in which the sacred and the profane, the real and the miraculous, were combined. Chagall could hardly have had a background better suited to his particular talents.
Above:
Marc Chagall as an adolescent in Vitebsk.

VIEW OF VITEBSK ♦
Marc Chagall, *View from the Window in Vitebsk*, 1908; St. Petersburg, Gordeyeva Collection. This is one of Chagall's earliest works, painted from the window of his house.

VITEBSK ♦ REMEMBERED
Marc Chagall, *I and the Village*, 1911-12; New York, MOMA. In this view of Vitebsk, painted in Paris, various memories of the city appear together like pieces in a kaleidoscope.

♦ HOUSES
The houses were often built from logs and had a courtyard.

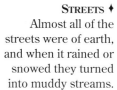

STREETS ♦
Almost all of the streets were of earth, and when it rained or snowed they turned into muddy streams.

♦ **FIRE**
On the day that
Chagall was born, a
fire forced the family
to flee the city.

♦ **THE GREAT
SYNAGOGUE**
This was the largest
and oldest of more
than sixty synagogues
in the city.

♦ **THE CHAGALL
FAMILY**
Marc Chagall
(standing on the left)
in a photograph taken
when he was young.

JUDAISM ♦
Marc Chagall, *The
Rabbi of Vitebsk*, 1914;
Venice, Museo d'Arte
Moderna. Rabbis
were important in the
religious and social
life of Vitebsk.
Chagall painted
several versions of
this composition.

CHAGALL'S LIFE

1. *Moshe Zakharovich Shagal (later Marc Chagall) was born
on July 7, 1887, in a suburb of Vitebsk, in Belarus, which was
at that time part of Russia. He was the first of nine children in
a Hasidic Jewish family. His grandfather David was a rabbi
and head of a municipal school. His father, Zakhar, was a
herring vendor, and often kept from his family by this work. His
mother, Feiga-Ita, both ran the household and managed a
small grocery store. It was she who bribed the teacher in order
to enroll Moshe in the local public school, to which Jews were
not usually admitted. Here he learned to speak Russian instead
of Yiddish and came into contact with middle-class life.* ⇒→

St. Petersburg

The atmosphere in St. Petersburg at the beginning of the 20th century, when Nicholas II was Tsar, was one of cultural upheaval and social tension – a result of the city's contact with the intellectual movements of more advanced countries in Europe. St. Petersburg was a cosmopolitan city where many foreign businesses had their offices. Modern industries were also based there, although the workers could only just survive on the wages these paid. While Moscow embodied the more traditional side of the Russian character, St. Petersburg, with its grand squares and thoroughfares, was a "window onto Europe". It was not unlike Paris, with painting, fashion, and theater playing an important role in the city's life. Famous painters regularly designed sets for the Imperial Theater, and it was through theater that Russian culture was able to make its greatest impact on the rest of Europe.

♦ **The Hermitage**
The bust above, by Bartolomeo Rastrelli, 1723-29, is of Tsar Peter the Great, who founded St. Petersburg as his capital in 1703.
In the center of the city, by the Neva River, the Winter Palace was built as the main residence of the Russian Tsars. Today it is known as the State Hermitage Museum, or simply the Hermitage, one of the most important museums of art in the world. It houses works by the greatest masters of European painting, including Leonardo da Vinci, Michelangelo, Velazquez, Caravaggio, El Greco, and Rembrandt. The art collection really began with Catherine II, who reigned from 1762 to 1796. Wanting to keep up with the fashion of the time for art collecting, she sought the advice of some of the major thinkers of the Enlightenment – most notably Voltaire and Diderot – to help her acquire works from all over Europe. By 1765, a new wing had to be added to the Winter Palace, to house all the new acquisitions. It was called the Pavillon de l'Hermitage (the Hermitage Pavilion), and today this part of the museum still houses Catherine II's collections.
The Hermitage is Russia's largest museum.

Shop signs ♦
Chagall paints a café sign. Work now given to designers and graphic artists used to be carried out by painters who, at a contractor's request, would devise and execute images and text for advertising purposes.

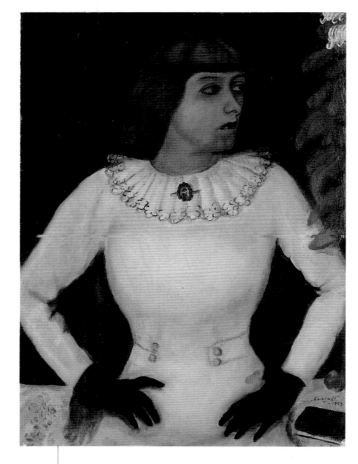

♦ **The fiancée**
Marc Chagall, *My Fiancée Wearing Black Gloves*, 1909; Basel, Kunstsammlung. This painting of Bella Rosenfeld, whom Chagall met in 1909, is one of his earliest portraits. The frontal view of the subject, and its central positioning, are traditional, but the placing of the hands and the head turned to the side give the picture a snapshot-like immediacy.

♦ **AT THE BALLET**
Léon Bakst, design for the *Great Eunuch,* 1910; Strasbourg, Musée des Beaux Arts.
Like many other painters of the period, Chagall's master Léon Bakst designed sets and costumes for the ballet.

♦ **ARCHITECTURE**
The dome of St. Catherine's Church, an elegant Baroque building, rises above the Neo-classical façades.

♦ **NEVSKY PROSPEKT**
The 2.5-mile-long Nevsky Prospekt runs southeastward from the Winter Palace square and is lined with fine buildings: palaces, churches, department stores, and theaters.

SHOP WINDOW ♦
A St. Petersburg shop window in a watercolor by Mstislav Dobuzhinsky. *The Hairdresser's Shop Window,* 1906; Moscow, Tretyakov Gallery.

2. CHAGALL'S LIFE ♦ *In 1907, when he was only twenty years old, Moshe succeeded in obtaining the permit that Jews required to live in the capital St. Petersburg. In Vitebsk, he had already studied with the local artist Yehuda Pen. Now, in St. Petersburg, at the Imperial School for the Promotion of the Arts, he hoped to acquire the advanced training that was not available at home. Life in the capital was not easy, and the young man eked out his living by painting shop signs. In 1908, he attended a school established by Elizaveta Zvantseva, an aristocrat who supported young artists. Among his teachers were Léon Bakst and Mstislav Dobuzhinsky; fellow students included the dancer Nijinsky and Countess Tolstoy. During one of his frequent trips to Vitebsk, Moshe met Bella Rosenfeld, who later became his wife.* ⇒♦

SELF-PORTRAITS

♦ **JOYFUL**
A detail from Marc Chagall, *The Promenade,* 1917-18; St. Petersburg, Russian Museum.

♦ **THE WORK**
Marc Chagall, *Self-Portrait*, 1908; oil on canvas, 30 x 24.5 cm. (11.8 x 9.6 in.); Grenoble, Musée de Peinture et de Sculpture. The story of Chagall's life can be traced through his self-portraits: for example, the early ones, when he was eager to make his debut as an artist; the joyous ones of 1914-20, when he returned to Vitebsk; and those painted in his assured, later years. The numerous self-portraits show us the artist in many different aspects: in front of his easel with palette and brushes in hand, during a pause from his work, or blissfully flying over the city and countryside. Sometimes Chagall portrayed himself with his head upside-down or being carried like an idol, as in the *Introduction to the Jewish Theater* (page 38). He was unusual in paying such attention to self-portraiture, which was no longer a popular genre in the 20th century. For centuries it had been considered one of the most important genres, demanding great skill and psychological insight, but now it was replaced by photography.

In his self-portrait of 1908, one of the first of many, Chagall portrays himself up close. Emerging from an area of shadow, he turns toward the observer. He seems to want to introduce himself, although somewhat tentatively, and therefore he has lowered the red mask that he has perhaps been wearing until a moment ago. The artist's head, with his long hair reaching the nape of his neck, occupies almost the entire canvas: Chagall portrays himself from a very short distance away, as though he has come so close in order to study himself and at the same time find a way to present himself to others.

♦ **STUDY**
Marc Chagall, *Self-Portrait*, 1907; Paris, Musée National d'Art Moderne. Here

Chagall portrays himself with his head turned slightly to the side and his gaze fixed on the observer.

♦ **UPSIDE-DOWN**
Marc Chagall, *Self-Portrait with Head Upside-down*, 1918; Moscow, Tretyakov Gallery. This work

belongs to the period when Chagall often portrayed himself flying. Here, a village appears through the clouds on the right.

The 1908 self-portrait belongs to the great tradition of self-portraiture, from Raphael and Titian to such 19th-century Russian painters as Repin. However, while Chagall followed the traditional approach of showing the face close-up, occupying the entire canvas, he also modernized it to some extent, by using a new

technique. Choosing not to represent himself in precise detail, he used broad brushstrokes to spread the paint thickly in some places while thinning it out over the canvas in others. He also left some parts of the painting in their initial stage as though, by avoiding descriptiveness, he could better capture the spirit of the subject.

♦ **FLYING**
Marc Chagall, *Over the Town*, 1914-18 (detail); Moscow, Tretyakov Gallery. The artist portrays himself flying, as though he is being carried along by the wind. The intense, impenetrable expression seems to emphasize the concentration required for this adventure.

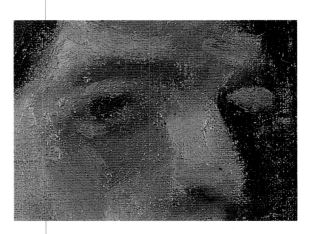

♦ **THE MODEL**
Titian, *Portrait of a Man*, c.1515; London, National Gallery. This greatly admired work is thought by many to be a portrait of the Italian poet Ariosto. Chagall's 1908 *Self-Portrait* seems to have borrowed ideas from the painting: the face emerging from the shadow, the hair falling along the nape of the neck, the sense of mystery.

A LATER EXAMPLE ♦
Marc Chagall, *Self-Portrait*, 1959-68; Florence, Uffizi. The bride, the fantastical bird, and the view of Notre-Dame in Paris in the background represent a compendium of the themes of Chagall's work. In this self-portrait from his later years, the artist's expression is tranquil.

♦ **SIMILARITIES**
A comparison of the eyes in Titian's *Portrait of a Man* with those in Chagall's 1908 *Self-Portrait* shows the similarities in approach of the two artists. Clearly Titian's painting was a model that the young Chagall hoped to emulate.

♦ **IN GREEN**
Marc Chagall, *Self-Portrait in Green*, 1914; Paris, Musée National d'Art Moderne. Painted during the years of his return to Vitebsk, this self-portrait owes its title to the color of the artist's close-fitting shirt or tunic.

PAINTING IN RUSSIA

The social and political situation was tense in Russia at the beginning of the 20th century. Nevertheless, the search for novelty in the arts continued, greatly stimulated by the passion and far-sightedness of several private collectors. Indeed, the cultural scene had never been as lively. Traditionalist painters such as Vrubel, who appears to have drawn his inspiration from ancient icons, and Kustodiev, whose hallmark was his realism, worked side by side with such artists as Goncharova, Larionov, and Malevich, who were clearly inspired by the European avant-garde, and Kandinsky, who was shortly to paint the first abstract watercolor, in Munich. There was both a desire to return to Russian origins and a great openness to new European influences and it was from the confrontation between these two impulses that modern Russian art was born.

♦ **ICONS**
The word icon comes from the Greek and simply means image. However, it came to refer in particular to a sacred image, which was often portable or placed above an altar. Russian icons were inspired by Byzantine models. At the beginning of the 11th century, the Byzantine style and technique of icon painting were imported into Russia and then handed down virtually unchanged until the 19th century. Sometimes these paintings on wooden or copper boards, or on canvas glued to wood, were covered with gold or silver leaf, except for the face, hands, and feet of the subjects.
During the 14th and 15th centuries, the monasteries of Kiev, Vladimir, and Novgorod were centers of famous icon painting schools.
One celebrated icon painter was Andrei Rublev (c.1360-1430), who introduced a new naturalism to his work.
Two Russian icons are shown here: above: *The Tranfiguration of Christ,* 1403 (detail); below: *Madonna and Child,* 13th century; Moscow, Tretyakov Gallery.

♦ **VRUBEL**
Mikhail Vrubel, *Six-Winged Seraph,* 1904; St. Petersburg, Russian Museum.

Vrubel's highly refined painting recalls the intricate decoration of ancient Orthodox churches.

♦ **GONCHAROVA**
Natalia Goncharova, *The Bleaching of the Canvas,* 1908; St. Petersburg, Russian Museum. Peasant women spread their wash on the grass to bleach it in the sun. Gonchavora's work was in complete contrast to Vrubel's. The quick, hard brushstrokes give an effect like a wood-engraving.

♦ **ICONOSTASIS**
In Orthodox churches, the sanctuary (where the altar is) is usually separated from the nave (where the worshipers sit). The screen, pillars, or railing separating the two areas is called the iconostasis. Sacred images (icons) on it face the worshipers.

✦ KUSTODIEV
Boris Kustodiev,
Carnival, 1916;
St. Petersburg,
Russian Museum.
The cart is having
difficulty driving

through the snow-
covered countryside.
A typical Russian city,
with its domes and
spires, can be seen
in the background
below.

✦ COLLECTING
Art collectors greatly
encouraged the
renewal of Russian
painting. The country
had very few public
institutions that
sponsored the arts.
(The art school
Chagall attended in
St. Petersburg
was private.)
Therefore, in Russia
more than anywhere
else, patrons and
collectors were
essential to young
artists.
In Moscow, two
private collections in
particular – those
owned by Sergei
Shchukin and
Ivan Morozov –
played the role that
contemporary art
exhibitions and
salons played
elsewhere.
At the outbreak of the
First World War,
Shchukin's collection
numbered more than
200 Impressionist and
Post-Impressionist
paintings, plus 50
canvases by Matisse
and Picasso. These
two artists even had
their own room in
his residence, which
they furnished
themselves.
Morozov owned
paintings by Monet,
Cézanne, and Renoir.
The homes of these
two collectors, which
were open to the
public on Saturdays,
were like a school to
many artists.
Above:
Sergei Shchukin.
Below: Ivan Morozov.

✦ OLD TESTAMENT
In the first two rows
of icons, the Old
Testament patriarchs
and prophets are
portrayed.

✦ NEW TESTAMENT
The center row
usually includes
images of Christ,
the Virgin Mary,
St. John the Baptist,
and scenes from
the Gospels.

✦ LOCAL ICONS
The lower part of
the iconostasis is
devoted to the Virgin
Mary, local saints or
festivals, and
guardian angels.

✦ KANDINSKY
Wassily Kandinsky,
A Red Church, 1908;
St. Petersburg,
Russian Museum.

Images from the
artist's childhood in
Russia appear in his
painting of the church
reflected in the lake.

✦ SEPARATION
In this example, there
is a railing in front of
the iconostasis, and
the iconostasis has a
center door. The

separation of the
sanctuary from
the nave is a
characteristic that
goes back to early
Christian churches.

PARIS IN 1910

Paris in the early 20th century was unparalleled as a gathering place for artists. Shockingly new painting styles were established by groups such as the Cubists, Symbolists, Fauvists, and Futurists. Art patrons and dealers revolved around them, and poets and writers were also drawn in. Controversial group exhibitions, public readings, and experimental plays caused great excitement and even scandal. Whereas, in the days of the Impressionists, Montmartre had become a lively artists' quarter, now the favorite meeting place was the calmer Montparnasse, on the left bank of the Seine River and farther away from the center of the city. Here, an extraordinary residential compound attracted artists like bees to a hive. It was called La Ruche, which means "beehive".

♦ LA RUCHE
In 1900, the Paris World's Fair was held at the edge of Montparnasse, in the wild fields beyond the rue de Vaugirard. One of the buildings created for the event was a strange, three-story, circular pavilion, designed to house the wine exhibition. After the show, the pavilion was purchased for a modest sum by the sculptor Alfred Boucher, who turned it into an artists' residence. It was divided up into studios, and the courtyard and surrounding area were filled with small houses and shacks. Everything was connected by stairways and passages.
Rents were very low, and among the first tenants were the artists Modigliani and Léger; then came many political refugees, among them Lenin, Trotsky, and Lunacharsky, and Russian artists, including Stravinsky, Archipenko, Zadkine, and Soutine. The last to arrive was Chagall. Artists could live on little at La Ruche ("the beehive"). The caretaker's family even provided cooked meals upon request, sometimes in exchange for paintings. A theater was created, and the residents also handwrote and illustrated a Jewish art journal called *Makhmaudim*.

Above:
a photograph of
La Ruche.

THE BEEHIVE ♦
Twelve studios were reached via the wooden staircase in the center of the circular building. The pavilion had a kind of honeycomb structure.

THE STUDIOS ♦
Each studio was shaped like a trapezoid, widening toward the window. There was a workroom equipped with a heater, and a loft for the bed.

THE METRO ♦
Gino Severini, *North-South*, 1912; Milan, Brera. The Italian painter Severini belonged to the Futurist movement. This painting represents Paris Metro stations.

♦ THE IMPRESSIONISTS' QUARTER
Maurice Utrillo, *View of Montmartre*, c.1910; Paris, Musée National d'Art Moderne. Montmartre, where the Impressionists had met, was now left to the tourists.

TWO CITIES ♦
Marc Chagall, *Self-Portrait with Seven Fingers*, 1912-13; Amsterdam, Stedelijk Museum. In this self-portrait, Chagall included images of his two most beloved cities: Vitebsk in the painting on the easel, and Paris outside the window of his studio.

♦ ADMIRERS
Marc Chagall, *Homage to Apollinaire,* 1911-12; Eindhoven, Stedelijk Van Abbemuseum.

Around the heart, Chagall included the names of four of his early supporters: Apollinaire, Cendrars, Canudo, and Walden.

♦ ADDED ON
Studios for the many artists who continued to arrive at La Ruche were built against the walls of the main building.

♦ THE ENTRANCE
The richly decorated entrance was a reminder of the building's original use as an exhibition hall.

3. CHAGALL'S LIFE ♦ *Léon Bakst, Moshe's teacher, moved to Paris to work for Diaghilev's Ballets Russes, and Moshe soon followed. It was 1910, the year of the World's Fair, and although Moshe knew no one and spoke no French, the city, which he called "my second Vitebsk", had a strong impact upon him. He visited the Louvre and all of the art galleries. At first he took a studio in the Impasse du Maine, but in the winter of 1911 he moved to La Ruche, the artists' colony in Montparnasse. It was in Paris that he changed his name to Marc Chagall. Slowly, he made friends: the poets Cendrars and Canudo, the painters Delaunay and Soutine, and, lastly, the prophet of contemporary art, the poet and art critic Apollinaire. When he first saw Chagall's paintings, in 1912, he is said to have murmured "Surnaturel".* ⇒♦

TO RUSSIA, ASSES, AND OTHERS

Strange figures suspended in space stand out against a night sky streaked with glowing lights. A red cow is on the roof of a house, suckling a calf and a green child. The dome of a church closely resembles that of Vitebsk. The woman hovering overhead is wearing a dress decorated with peacock eyes, and her head is detached from her body. Such fantastical visions are a particular feature of Chagall's works; however, in painting them, he and his contemporaries, such as Altman, were following a Russian tradition that had begun in the late 19th century with Petrov-Vodkin.

✦ **THE WORK**
Marc Chagall,
To Russia, Asses, and Others, 1911-12;
oil on canvas,
156 x 122 cm.
(61.5 x 48 in.);
Paris, Musée National d'Art Moderne.
This large work was among the first that Chagall painted in his new and more spacious studio at La Ruche, to which he had moved from the Impasse du Maine. The painting was included in an exhibition at the Salon des Indépendants in March 1912.
Its curious title had been suggested by the artist's friend, the poet Blaise Cendrars, and Chagall liked it very much; the enigmatic title suited the intriguing nature of the painting.
The work created quite a stir at the Salon because it seemed both naive and complex at the same time and was very different from the other paintings on show.
Speaking about it, Chagall mentioned his childhood in Vitebsk and the cows that he heard at dawn from the slaughterhouses near La Ruche: "Somewhere not far away they start cutting the throats of the cattle, cows bellow and I paint them."
Above:
a realistic detail: the metal bucket is not simply floating but seems to slip from the woman's hand.

✦ **A PAINTING OF A PAINTING**
A detail from *Self-Portrait with Seven Fingers,* 1912-13; Amsterdam, Stedelijk Museum. In this painting (shown whole on page 15), Chagall included a small version of *To Russia, Asses, and Others,* on the artist's easel.

A fantastical vision characterizes Chagall's painting from his earliest works, whether they be actual views or memories of Vitebsk. However, To Russia and other paintings completed in Paris in 1910-13 stand out as examples of this tendency. Perhaps his distance from home was distorting his memories; but also the new painting styles that he saw around him – from that of Delaunay to the Cubists – inspired him to work more freely, following his feelings.

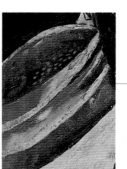

✦ **PEOPLE AND OBJECTS**
All the elements of the picture – people, animals, and objects – seem equally alive.
Above: the child and the animal sucking milk; left: the tub seems to move as if it were animate.

♦ PETROV-VODKIN
Kuzma Petrov-Vodkin, *Red Horse Bathing,* 1912; Moscow, Tretyakov Gallery.
In the late 19th and early 20th centuries, the Russian artist Petrov-Vodkin painted fantastic animals, such as these red horses, and unreal events in mythological settings.

A SYMBOL ♦
Marc Chagall, *The Red Horse*, 1938-44; Nantes, Musée des Beaux-Arts. Chagall's fantastic animals are not only creatures inhabiting an enchanted world. On occasion they are symbols. For example, this horse evokes the fearful atmosphere of war. The strength of this work lies in the contrast of red with blue and green.

♦ANIMALS
Marc Chagall, *Introduction to the Jewish Theater*, 1920 (detail); Moscow, Tretyakov Gallery. When Chagall includes goats and cows and other animals in scenes involving people, he gives them human expressions and physical attitudes.

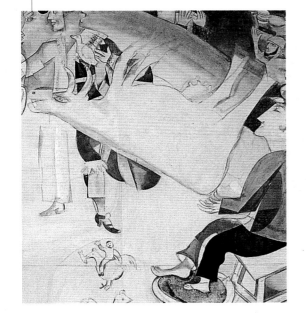

IN HARMONY ♦
Marc Chagall, *Solitude*, 1933; Tel Aviv, Art Museum. The heifer, with its large, wide-open eye and solemn expression, and the violin that it is playing with its mouth, seems to be in harmony with the melancholy of the Jew and the angel floating above.

BALLETS RUSSES

Considered sophisticated and yet exotic and barbaric, Russia was in vogue in Paris in the early 20th century. This was largely due to Russian promoter of the arts Sergei Diaghilev. In 1909 he opened a season of Ballets Russes (Russian ballets) at the Châtelet Theater. Ballet boasted a long tradition in Russia, but Diaghilev's production was something new: he had chosen excerpts from several ballets for their spectacular acrobatic element and deep emotion, and he designed costumes and sets to highlight their particular Russian character. Whereas traditional ballet was a showcase for the solo dancers' technical skills, Diaghilev saw all aspects of the performance as equally important: stage design, choreography, music, singing, and dancing all combined as "total art" – which was a favored concept at this time. Chagall was not actively involved, but it was partly owing to the Russian vogue that his painting now became better understood.

✦ SERGEI DIAGHILEV
(1872-1929)
Sergei Diaghilev was born in Novgorod. He went to study Law in St. Petersburg, and there he met the painters Benois and Bakst, who later became designers for his ballet productions. Also in St. Petersburg he founded an art journal and served as artistic manager of the Imperial Theater, from which he was ousted for favoring his protégés too openly. He was superstitious and snobbish, and determined to achieve success. Above all, he was a formidable organizer of other people's work. After his expulsion from the Imperial Theater, he explored many different avenues. In 1905, he organized an exhibition of 18th-century Russian portraits at the Tauride Palace. This was a genre of painting which was unknown to most and generally dismissed as primitive. In 1906, he left Russia for Paris, where, at the Salon d'Automne, held in the Grand Palais, he set up a major exhibition of Russian art from medieval icons to contemporary painting. The exhibition included 750 works by approximately 50 artists and was displayed in 13 halls decorated by Léon Bakst. Having founded the Ballets Russes in 1909, Diaghilev toured with the company in Europe and the Americas. He died in Venice.

NIJINSKY ✦
From a distance, Vassily Nijinsky greets his friend Chagall, with whom he attended Léon Bakst's painting lessons in St. Petersburg.

✦ PORTRAIT
Léon Bakst, *Portrait of Sergei Diaghilev*, 1906; St. Petersburg, Russian Museum.

✦ D'ANNUNZIO
The Italian poet Gabriele d'Annunzio meets the dancer Ida Rubinstein at the Châtelet Theater. His work, *The Martyrdom of St. Sebastian,* for which Debussy wrote the score, will be dedicated to her.

✦ PRIMA BALLERINA
Anna Pavlova, the female star of the Ballets Russes.

BACKDROP ✦
Alexander Golovin,
backdrop design for
Boris Godunov, 1907;
Moscow, Bakhrushin
State Central
Theatrical Museum.

✦ SET DESIGN
Léon Bakst, stage
design for the ballet
Schéhérazade, 1910;
Paris, Musée des
Arts Décoratifs.

COSTUME ✦
Léon Bakst, design
for the costume of
Narcissus, 1911;
London, The Fine
Arts Society.

✦ IMPRESARIO
All phases of the
preparation are
supervised by
Diaghilev, who is
here asking the
opinion of Picasso.

**✦ A MEETING
BETWEEN MASTER
AND PUPIL**
Bakst (front left)
shows his former
pupil Chagall some
of his sketches for
set designs.

4. CHAGALL'S LIFE ✦ *Chagall went to see the Ballets Russes at the Châtelet Theater, as did half of Paris, but he was also allowed to watch rehearsals. There he met old friends, such as the dancer Nijinsky, who had attended painting classes with him in St. Petersburg; and his former teacher, Léon Bakst, now stage designer for the ballet. Chagall was not overly impressed by ballets, although he described them as "worldly, charming, and sparkling"; but he wanted to create some set designs and so he invited Bakst to see his new paintings. The teacher went to Chagall's studio in the Impasse du Maine, observed everything and commented, "Now, your colors sing"; but he did not offer any work. More positively, when Chagall's paintings were exhibited at the Salon des Indépendants in 1912, they were well received. It was on that occasion that Apollinaire introduced Chagall to the art dealer Herwarth Walden. Walden proposed an exhibition in Berlin.* ➠

BEYOND CUBISM

The works of Picasso and Braque and their artistic movement, Cubism, may be the most well-known examples of early 20th-century art, but the art scene in Paris at that time was in fact quite varied; many styles developed alongside Cubism, as well as in reaction to it. Painters including Gris and Léger continued along the Cubist path, while others pursued the idea of a return to the great tradition of figure-painting. Of the latter, Matisse and de Chirico were the key figures. Analytical Cubism and realism represented the two extreme positions. Between them were many other styles. For example, Delaunay and Kupka, who had started as Cubists, created essentially color-based works and moved toward completely abstract art. Duchamp thought of painting as provocation, absurdity, a reversal of the usual ways of thinking about things. And others regarded it as pure rhythm (Modigliani) or as a celebration of progress (Boccioni.)

◆ DEVELOPING CUBISM
A growing number of artists took up and developed the Cubist style. Its basis was the simultaneous representation of reality from many points of view.
1. Pablo Picasso, *The Poet*, 1911; and
2. Georges Braque, *The Clarinet*, 1912; both in Venice, Peggy Guggenheim Collection.
3. Juan Gris, *The Three Cards*, 1913; Berne, Kunstmuseum.
4. Fernand Léger, *Woman in Blue*, 1912; Basel, Kunstmuseum.

◆ BEGINNING
Pablo Picasso, *Les Demoiselles d'Avignon*, 1907; New York, MOMA. This is the painting by Picasso that paved the way for Cubism.

◆ THE GRAND TRADITION
At the opposite extreme from the Cubists, with their theories and scientific approach, were those artists who sought to renew the great tradition of figure-painting.
1. Henri Matisse, *Luxury II*, 1907; Copenhagen, Statens Museum for Kunst.
2. Henry Matisse, *Interior with Eggplants*, 1911; Grenoble, Musée de Peinture.
3. Giorgio de Chirico, *The Enigma of the Hour*, 1911; Milan, private collection.

◆ BOCCIONI
Umberto Boccioni, *The City Rises*, 1910; New York, MOMA. Boccioni was part of the Italian Futurist movement, which aimed to produce dynamic, modern works and to find ways of representing time and movement.

NEW MOVEMENTS ◆
The art movements that developed in the early 20th century were very different from each other.
1. Frantisek Kupka, *Verticals*, 1911-12 (detail); Paris, Musée National d'Art Moderne.
2. Marcel Duchamp, *Nude Descending a Staircase no. 1*, 1911; Philadelphia, Museum of Art.
3. Robert Delaunay, *The City*, 1910; Paris, Musée National d'Art Moderne.
4. Amedeo Modigliani, *Head*, 1911-12; London, The Tate Gallery.

2

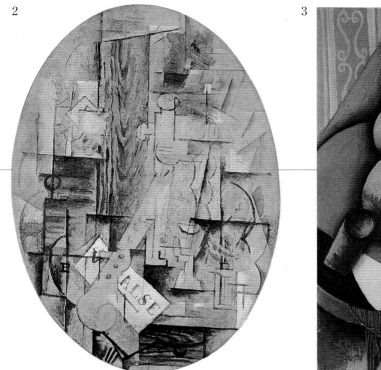

3

4

2

3

2

3

4

THE VIOLINIST

The large violinist with a green face seems more like a figure from a dream than a real person. He is so tall that, if he were to stand straight, his head would stretch beyond the top of the canvas. The curved green and yellow area on which he is standing can be interpreted as the planet earth, surrounded by the blackness of space. On the right is a blossoming tree, full of birds. The roofs of the houses are covered with snow and between them, at the very top of the picture, a golden angel is passing by in the sky. It was a tradition in Hasidic communities for a violinist to play at birth celebrations, weddings, and funerals. In many of Chagall's paintings, the violinist became a mythical figure, a kind of guardian angel.

♦ **THE WORK**
The Violinist,
1912-13,
oil on canvas,
188 x 158 cm. (74 x
62 in.); Amsterdam,
Stedelijk Museum.
This painting can be
likened in many ways
to *To Russia, Asses,
and Others:*
it was painted in the
new and more
spacious studio in
La Ruche, it was
particularly dear
to Chagall, and it
was shown
at the Salon des
Indépendants, this
time in 1914.
Like *To Russia,
The Violinist*
attracted a great deal
of attention, and its
success was such
that a drawing
reproducing it was
featured prominently
in the German art
journal *Der Sturm*,
at the same time as
an exhibition of
Chagall's work took
place in the journal's
gallery in Berlin.
The Violinist, which
was preceded by a
small gouache
version of 1912
and followed by the
large *Green Violinist*
of 1923, should be
considered the most
representative
of the series.
While violinists
appear frequently
in Chagall's work,
they are rarely the
main subject: rather,
they tend to be
marginal figures,
sometimes flying.
In the 1930s,
Chagall also began
to paint animal
violinists.

Above:
a detail showing
the violinist's face.

♦ **ONLOOKERS**
At the bottom left-hand side of the painting, we notice the profiled heads of three children, who are looking up toward the violinist's face. Their small size makes the violinist seem, by contrast, even more of a gigantic figure.

THE ANGEL ♦
In the sky behind the violinist's head a golden angel flies between the roofs of two houses. This detail adds a further mystical touch to a scene that is dominated by fantasy.

In the paintings of his early years in Paris, Chagall devoted himself to reconstructing his memories of his Russian homeland. The Violinist, like the others, is a kaleidoscope of images all presented together, according to the Cubist vision. But in this case, compared with the others, such as To Russia, Asses, and Others, *the composition is much more compact: the different elements seem designed to fit together like pieces of a jigsaw puzzle.*

♦ **HANDS**
In his figure drawing, Chagall was more concerned with expressing character than with achieving anatomical accuracy.

♦ A MEMORY
A detail from *The Green Violinist*, 1923. In this later painting, Chagall replaced the three children in *The Violinist* with the figure of a man holding a kind of small shovel. As before, the very small figure accentuates the size of the violinist.

RUSSIAN WEDDING ♦
Marc Chagall, *The Wedding*, 1909; Zurich, Bührle Foundation. Chagall painted this picture of a wedding procession, with a violinist leading, while he was in St. Petersburg, at Zvantseva's school.

♦ THE FLYING MAN
A detail from *The Green Violinist*, 1923. Compared with *The Violinist* of 1912-13, the tone here is calmer, the atmosphere less mysterious, and, instead of the golden angel in the sky between the houses, Chagall painted a man – flying.

♦ ACCOMPANIST
A detail from *The Wedding Candles*, 1945; Paris, private collection. In Chagall's world, musicians played at sad as well as happy occasions. Here a young man colored in green, and with a ghostly air, is playing a cello. He is at the head of a group of musicians, leading the sad procession of Bella's wedding-funeral.

♦ THE LATER WORK
Marc Chagall, *The Green Violinist*, 1923; New York, Solomon R. Guggenheim Museum.
There are many similarities between *The Violinist* of 1912-13 and this painting done ten years later. The main differences are that, in the later work, the composition is less crowded and there is no surface for the figure to stand on. The houses at the bottom seem to sink into space.

BERLIN, 1914

Avant-garde painting styles in Paris largely reflected Cubist ideas on rationality and structure – and therefore Chagall's works, whose content was so foreign to those ideas, caused astonishment at every exhibition in the city. In Berlin, however, the artistic climate was quite different. In the years before the First World War, many painters, from Grosz and Dix to Marc, developed a strongly expressive style. They often used violent colors and thick brushstrokes, taking their subjects from modern city life, including beggars and unscrupulous profiteers. They also sensed the coming of the war, which they saw as the ultimate folly of a corrupt society. Some dreamed of a return to basic spiritual values. In this climate, Chagall's work, with its strong vein of fantasy, was received with interest from its first appearance in 1914.

♦ **EXPRESSIONISM**
Expressionism developed in the early 20th century, in opposition to realist painting and the serene style of the Impressionists, who had focused their attention on representing the outside world. Drawing their inspiration from Van Gogh and Munch, Expressionist artists sought rather to express the inner world; and their discomfort with contemporary civilization, which was on the verge of world war, meant that their work was characterized by distorted forms and violently contrasting colors.
In 1905, in Dresden, Germany, three architecture students, Kirchner, Heckel, and Schmidt-Rottluff, formed a group called Die Brücke (the bridge; their work was intended to be a bridge to the art of the future).
From then until about 1930, Expressionism was the main form of art in Germany. The Dresden group moved to Berlin in 1910 and then disbanded in 1913. However, their ideas created a cultural movement that had its equivalents not only in painting but also in music (Schönberg), fiction (Kafka), and drama (Brecht.)

Above:
Otto Dix, *War*, 1914 (detail); Düsseldorf, Kunstmuseum.

♦ **CITY SCENE**
George Grosz, *Metropolis*, 1916-17; Lugano, Thyssen-Bornemisza

Collection. Crowds of people throng a city which is lit by a sinister reddish light.

5. CHAGALL'S LIFE ♦ *In 1914, after four years in Paris, Chagall departed for Berlin, where Herwarth Walden had organized an exhibition of his work in the gallery of the art journal* Der Sturm. *This was the artist's first significant solo exhibition and made Chagall doubly happy because it was also an enormous success. Franz Marc and Paul Klee, who had already seen his work in Paris, helped him to sell several paintings. Among them was* Golgotha, *which was purchased by Koehler, an art collector and patron of a number of artists, including Wassily Kandinsky. Richer now than he had ever been, Chagall decided to travel to Russia – to return to Vitebsk, of course, and to his fiancée Bella.* ➤♦

♦ **STREET SCENE**
George Grosz, *The Street*, 1915; Stuttgart, Staatsgalerie. The moon casts its light from a blood-red sky onto scenes of urban degradation. The houses seem to be on the verge of collapsing.

THE BUYER ♦
Bernard Koehler listens with interest to a group of artists praising Chagall.

♦ **ON THE TERRACE**
The artists associated with the journal *Der Sturm* usually gathered on a terrace that looked out on the city of Berlin. The gallery owner and art critic Herwarth. Walden presides.

MARC CHAGALL ♦
The artist in Berlin for his first solo exhibition.

♦ **SOLD**
Marc Chagall,
Golgotha, 1912;
New York, MOMA.
The dramatic
atmosphere and
strange, distorted
figures in this
painting are
reminiscent of the
Expressionists,
despite its cubistic
elements.

OSKAR KOKOSCHKA ♦
A painter and editor
of the journal
Der Sturm, he
regularly attended
Walden's gatherings.

ERWARTH WALDEN ♦
Herwarth Walden
ows Chagall's work
to a prospective
buyer.

♦ **PROSTITUTES**
Ernst Ludwig
Kirchner,
*Five Women
on the Street*,
1913; Cologne,
Museum Ludwig.
Kirchner intended
this painting of
prostitutes, with its
acid colors, sharp
brushstrokes, and
caricature-like
distortions, as a
denunciation of
modern society.

♦ **GUILLAUME
APOLLINAIRE**
The poet followed his
protégé Chagall to
Berlin.

♦ **NATURE**
Franz Marc, *The
Red Roe Deer*, 1912;
Munich, Staatsgalerie
Moderner Kunst.
The German painter
Marc believed that
animals were more
beautiful and spiritual
than people.

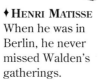

♦ **HENRI MATISSE**
When he was in
Berlin, he never
missed Walden's
gatherings.

♦ **RECOMMENDATION**
Paul Klee and Franz
Marc, two of
Chagall's admirers,
encourage the art
collector Koehler to
purchase *Golgotha*.

CHAGALL AND HIS FAMILY

Life in Vitebsk was a recurrent theme in Chagall's painting. However, the way in which he portrayed it changed completely during the period following his return home from Paris and Berlin in 1914. In place of his earlier fantasy scenes, he now produced works from direct observation, showing scenes as he actually saw them. His subjects included his parents' house, his uncle's store in Lyozno, his father in his prayer shawl on Jewish holidays, the interiors of synagogues, and detailed views of his garden and the Vitebsk skyline. In painting these, and also new subjects such as portraits of his daughter Ida, who was born in 1916, Chagall shows a new interest in recording actual details, as if to preserve the peace and joy of those days. Thus, his paintings during this period are almost like a diary. The fantastic, irrational component (as, for example, in *The Violinist*) gives way to a chronicling of facts and objects which are shown in a simple, straightforward manner.

♦ **THE SHOP**
Marc Chagall, *My Uncle's Store in Lyozno*, 1914; Moscow, Tretyakov Gallery.

♦ **OBJECTS**
Marc Chagall, *The Mirror*, 1915; St. Petersburg, Russian Museum. The mirror in which the oil lamp is reflected is giant-sized compared with the tiny figure at the bottom left. Everyday objects are given a mysterious aspect too.

♦ **PHOTOGRAPHIC VIEW**
Marc Chagall, *View from the Window in Vitebsk*, 1914-15; Moscow, Tretyakov Gallery. This is a realistic portrayal of a window in Chagall's house.

The oil lamp and the embroidered curtains and, outside, the view of the garden and the houses and churches of Vitebsk are shown in careful detail. The whole scene has the clarity of a photograph.

♦ **AN OLD MAN**
Marc Chagall, *The Red Jew*, 1914-15; St. Petersburg, Russian Museum. In this period, Chagall often portrayed visitors to his home – in particular elderly itinerant Jews. They are shown in different colors, suggesting their state of mind and mood.

♦ **MORNING SCENE**
Marc Chagall, *The Pink House*, or *The Street,* 1922; Paris, Musée d'Art Moderne de la Ville. This painting was a study for an illustration in Chagall's autobiography *Ma Vie* (My Life). It shows his father leaving the house in the morning for the synagogue.

THE EARLIER STYLE ♦
Pregnant Woman 1913; Amsterdam, Stedelijk Museum. This extraordinary painting from Chagall's Paris years is reminiscent of Leonardo da Vinci's anatomical drawings.

THE NEW STYLE ♦
The Mother in Front of the Oven, 1914; Paris, Ida Chagall Archives. One of Chagall's first paintings upon his return to Vitebsk, this domestic scene is realistic except for the little man at the woman's feet.

♦ **SYNAGOGUE**
Marc Chagall, *The Synagogue*, 1917; private collection. Chagall's family – particularly his father and his grandfather, who had been a rabbi – attended synagogue regularly. They viewed it as a kind of extension of their home. Therefore, paintings of the synagogue are as much a part of Chagall's domestic painting as are portraits of his wife and daughter.

6. CHAGALL'S LIFE ♦ *Chagall moved from Paris to Berlin and then, in 1914, to Vitebsk. His intention was to pay only a short visit, but the outbreak of war in 1914 and then the 1917 Russian Revolution turned it into a very long stay. He set up a studio near his father's house and painted whatever he saw around him. Bella's family, also Jewish, did not approve of a Jew working as a painter, but gradually Chagall overcame their resistance and in 1915 the couple were married at last. They moved to St. Petersburg where Chagall had obtained a government post, in a military office, in order to avoid being sent to the front. In 1916, their daughter Ida was born.* ⟫→

THE REVOLUTION IN RUSSIA

Discontent with the Tsar and his government had been mounting in Russia since the 19th century, and was intensified by the country's disastrous involvement in the First World War. Millions of Russians were sent to the front and both soldiers and those left at home suffered atrociously. In March 1917, following a great wave of strikes and demonstrations by soldiers and workers, Tsar Nicholas II abdicated. For the next few months, provisional governments of moderate socialists and liberals failed to end the unpopular war. Then they were swept away by the Bolsheviks, in an armed uprising on the night of November 6-7, 1918. The Bolsheviks were led by Vladimir Ilyich Ulianov, better known as Lenin. He became head of the first Soviet government and set about turning the Soviet Union (the new name for Russia) into a classless, Communist state.

♦ LENIN AS ACROBAT
Marc Chagall, a study for *The Revolution,* 1937 (whole, above and detail, left); Paris, Musée National d'Art Moderne. Lenin as an acrobat, with Russian citizens and soldiers as the spectators in a circus: this was Chagall's view of the revolution 20 years after. He later cut up the painting into three parts. Only this small oil study shows the original conception.

♦ MODERNISM
Vladimir Tatlin, Model for a monument to the Third International, 1919-20, (reconstruction); Stockholm, Moderna Museet. At first the Revolution encouraged modern art such as Tatlin's.

♦ A NEW WORLD
Konstantin Yuon, *Red Planet,* 1921; Moscow, Tretyakov Gallery. A work celebrating the victory of the Bolshevik Revolution.

♦ AT THE WINTER PALACE
The Winter Palace, the headquarters of the provisional government, fell into the hands of the Bolsheviks in November 1917.

PROPAGANDA ♦
Marc Chagall, a
sketch for a poster,
War on the Palaces,
1918-19; Moscow,
Tretyakov Gallery.
At first, Chagall was
caught up in the
revolutionary fever.

OVER VITEBSK

A deserted street: on the right, behind a low fence, is a large church, the cathedral of Vitebsk, with several houses clustered around it. Across the road from the church is another building enclosed by a tall fence. There is snow on the ground and the sky is gray. Silhouetted against the sky, as if rising slowly and quietly from behind the church, is the figure of an elderly Jew – a frequent subject of Chagall's paintings – with a walking stick and a bag slung over his shoulder. He is reminiscent of flying figures which appear both in ancient Russian icons and in the 13th- and 14th-century frescoes of Giotto and Simone Martini. They have a sense of "everyday miracle" about them, as if flying were a normal human activity.

♦ A STUDY
Chagall, *Over Vitebsk*, 1914; St. Petersburg, Simina Collection. This version is more detailed than the painting shown below. The difference can be seen in the church entrance, the snow on the roofs, and the fence posts.

♦ THE WORK
Over Vitebsk, 1915-20; oil on canvas, 67 x 92.7 cm. (26.5 x 36.5 in.), New York, MOMA. There are three versions of this painting, which Chagall probably created in St. Petersburg, while the First World War was raging in Europe and revolution was brewing in Russia. Clearly the wandering Jew was a subject that interested him, perhaps as a symbol of the Jewish experience.
Two of the versions, both painted in 1914, are in oils on cardboard, as were most of Chagall's paintings during this period, and were probably studies. The first is now in the Art Gallery of Ontario, Toronto, Canada, and the second in St. Petersburg.
The third version, reproduced as the main picture on this page, is housed in the Museum of Modern Art in New York.
The greatest difference between the two studies and the painting is the increased magical effect, in the painting, of the Jewish figure passing in the sky.
The absence of any other figures and the white light of the snow give a fantastical quality to the scene.

Above: a detail of the buildings.

The painting has the atmosphere of a fairy tale or a miracle story. The scene, with the figure flying across the sky, is presented from a point of view above the line of the horizon, so that the viewer also feels suspended in the void. Many common elements of Chagall's painting are included here: the street, the church, the snow-covered roofs; but they are brought together in a realistic landscape, in the context of which the floating figure seems all the more incongruous. It is the combination of the two different registers, the fantastic and the realistic, that gives the painting its astonishing effect.

♦ THE WANDERING JEW
Marc Chagall, *Over Vitebsk*, 1915-20 (detail). Perhaps the figure of a Jewish man in flight is a symbol of the Diaspora.

♦ GIOTTO

In 1290-95, Giotto painted a series of frescoes portraying the life of St. Francis, in the Upper Church of St. Francis at Assisi.

In the episode shown on the left, a mysterious (flying) chariot of fire enters the house, and everyone understands that the spirit of God has come among them. In the episode on the right, while praying, Francis is raised from the ground by a luminous cloud. The figure of Christ leans down to bless him.

SIMONE MARTINI ♦
Simone Martini, *The Blessed Agostino Novello and His Four Miracles*, 1325-28 (detail); Siena, Pinacoteca Nazionale. The saint is portrayed flying down from a cloud, like a swallow. He has appeared in order to save a child who has fallen from the first-floor balcony because of a broken floor-board.

♦ THE BYZANTINE TRADITION

The two icons shown here share a common subject: *Elijah's Fiery Ascension*, 16th century; Moscow, Tretyakov Gallery. The use of red and gold leaf was typical of Russian icons.

THE RETURN TO ORDER

In the years following his marriage in 1915, Chagall often portrayed himself and Bella. The paintings have a dream-like atmosphere, with the couple often shown as flying above the city of Vitebsk. In contrast, the backgrounds against which they are set are relatively realistic and substantial. Sometimes, as in *Bella with a White Collar*, the portrait of the artist's wife seems to have been inspired by ancient models. Many artists seemed to feel a need to return to the ideals of traditional, classical painting, perhaps in reaction to the catastrophe of the First World War. Yet, in an attempt to represent the chaos surrounding them, they also mixed the real with the unreal, painting statue-like figures in dream-like landscapes.

♦ **PICASSO**
Pablo Picasso, *The Race*, 1922; Paris, Picasso Museum.
Two women, with statue-like bodies, in a timeless landscape.

This is an example of the return to order. Picasso had been influenced by seeing the works of Giotto and Masaccio and the ancient paintings of Pompeii.

7. CHAGALL'S LIFE ♦ *In St. Petersburg Chagall was put in charge of the war-time propaganda office, but the daily routine depressed him and he did not have the makings of a bureaucrat. More positively, life in the capital – in spite of dire poverty (it snowed through the roof of the small room where he and Bella lived) – enabled him to meet several great poets, including Blok, Yesenin, Mayakovsky, and Pasternak, with whom he discussed art. Above all, he was able to take part in several important exhibitions. Some well-known art collectors bought his works, although at a very low price, and in 1918 the first monograph on his work was published. By then the Russian Revolution had taken place and the Bolsheviks were in power. In September 1918, Chagall was appointed Commissar for Art in Vitebsk, to which he and Bella had returned.* ➤

♦ **MARITAL BLISS**
Above left: *The Promenade*, 1917-18; St. Petersburg, Russian Museum.
Above: *Double Portrait with Wineglass*, 1917-18; Paris, Musée National d'Art Moderne.
Many paintings like these of Chagall and Bella express the artist's joy and happiness in his marriage. The couple seem weightless. In *The Promenade*, Bella is flown through the air like a kite. In the *Double Portrait with Wineglass* she is hovering above the river; and yet, at the same time, there is a sense of solidity in the way she seems to be stepping forward onto her right foot, as well as in the view of Vitebsk in the background, which looks like an 18th-century painting.

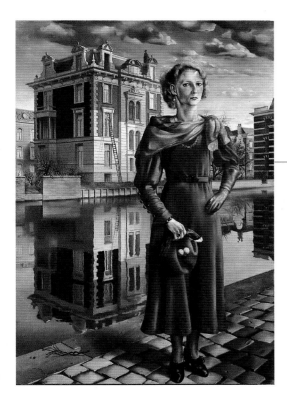

♦ **COMPARISONS**
Far left: A. Carel
Willink, *Wilma*, 1933;
The Hague,
Gemeentemuseum.
Left: Felice Casorati,
Silvana Cenni, 1922;
Turin, private
collection.
These two examples
of return to order,
from the Netherlands
and Italy, show
women in stiff, aloof
poses like those of
classical statues.
At the same time,
the women's
imposing presence,
or fixed, almost
hallucinatory gaze,
give the paintings an
air of mystery.

♦ **CLASSICAL**
Marc Chagall,
*Bella with a White
Collar*, 1917; Paris,
Musée National
d'Art Moderne.
Bella's large white
collar in this portrait
is reminiscent of a
Renaissance ruff.

♦ **IN FLIGHT**
Marc Chagall,
Over the Town,
1914-18; Moscow,
Tretyakov Gallery.
Another image of the
young couple flying
over Vitebsk. The
expressions of Marc
and Bella emphasize
their estrangement
from reality.

♦ **PORTRAITS**
Far left: Grant Wood,
American Gothic,
1930; Chicago,
The Art Institute.
Left: Giorgio de
Chirico, *Self-Portrait*,
1924; Toledo, Ohio,
Toledo Museum
of Art.
Portraits of this period
show a concern for
the durable and
eternal. Wood and
other American artists
often drew on local
traditions. De Chirico
here represents
himself as a statue.

CHAGALL AS ART EDUCATOR

In the optimistic climate following the overthrow of the old regime, Russian artists were given important responsibilities. The new revolutionary government had a vision of cultural education, based on an idea present in many early 20th-century art movements: that art could be an active force in the process of social change and could somehow bring about a new consciousness. Art schools and academies flourished. One was founded in Vitebsk, and Lenin, the leader of the government, and Lunacharsky, the Minister for Popular Culture, asked Chagall to be its director. They had met the artist in Paris, at La Ruche, and admired his work. One of his first tasks at the new Vitebsk Academy was to prepare the celebrations for the Revolution's second anniversary, in November 1919.

♦ CELEBRATIONS OF THE REVOLUTION
The years following the Revolution were hard for people in Russia, with fear, poverty, and serious unrest everywhere. Civil war between the Whites (who were against the Bolsheviks) and the Bolshevik Red Army went on until 1922. But there was also a feeling of great hope for the future, which helped make the difficulties seem smaller. The new leaders of the country realized that they must fuel that hope and reassure people that changes were being made. Therefore they devised celebrations of the Revolution, lasting several days and involving the entire population. City squares were filled, and buildings covered, with magnificent displays. Chagall was involved in preparing the celebrations in Vitebsk, where some 350 banners were hung, seven triumphal arches were built, and storefronts and trams were painted. The cost of all this (for which Chagall was not responsible) caused much controversy. Above and below: two studies by Chagall: *The Wounded Soldier*, 1914; Philadelphia, Museum of Art; *The Refugees*, 1914; Moscow, Tretyakov Gallery.

♦ RISING OF THE DEAD Marc Chagall, *The Cemetery*, 1917; Paris, Musée National d'Art Moderne. The cemeteries in Chagall's paintings after the Revolution symbolized the idea of rebirth. In one work, *Cemetery Gates*, he included words from the Bible announcing the resurrection of the dead, as a metaphor for the Revolution.

♦ CULTURAL REFORM "Art and culture for the people" was one of the revolutionaries' aims for the future. The contents of libraries were driven on carts around the streets, in an effort to reach new readers.

♦ DISPLAYS Everything was moved out on to the street for the anniversary celebration. For example, store owners set up improvised stands.

REDS AND WHITES ♦
This famous poster
designed by the
painter El Lissitzky in
1919 shows a red
wedge smashing into
a white circle, an
allusion to the
Communist
revolutionaries and
their enemies.

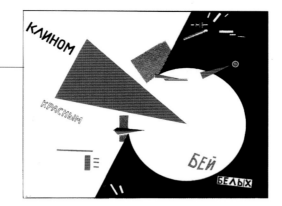

AGIT-PROP ♦
Artists created
slogans and designed
posters and costumes
for actors who
traveled across the
country, presenting
"living scenes" of the
Revolution.
Afterwards the
performers would
often hold
discussions with
the audience.

♦ MALEVICH
Kazimir Malevich,
*Suprematism no. 58
with Yellow and Black*,
1916; St. Petersburg,
Russian Museum.
Malevich and his
Suprematist
movement carried
abstraction to its
logical conclusion.
(See pages 36-37.)

FRIENDS ♦
Chagall converses
with his friend
Kazimir Malevich,
who founded the
Suprematist
movement in
Moscow in 1915.

8. CHAGALL'S LIFE ♦ *Chagall viewed the future in Vitebsk with optimism. The revolutionary government had given Jews equal rights with other Russian citizens. In February 1919 he became the director of a new art school, set up in a former banker's residence that had been seized by the revolutionaries. It was called the "Free Academy" and was inaugurated in a solemn ceremony during which the poet Pustinin read an ode in honor of Chagall. The artist had ambitious projects for the academy. The students worked in large collective studios where specialized craftsmen, such as colorists and decorators, served as assistants. The idea was to establish a brotherhood among artists and, to accomplish this, Chagall sought the help of El Lissitzky, Ivan Puni, and Kazimir Malevich. Exhibitions, shows, and debates were organized.* ⇒♦

THE IMPACT OF ABSTRACT PAINTING

♦ **KANDINKSY**
(1866-1944)
Wassily Kandinsky
(above), was about
ten years older than
Chagall; he was also
Russian-born, but
moved to Germany
before the end of the
19th century and
eventually became
first a German and
then a French citizen.
He created his first
abstract work, *First
Abstract Watercolor*,
in Munich in 1910.

While abstract
patterns had been
used as decoration
since ancient times,
Kandinsky's work
was quite different, in
that he intentionally
entrusted shapes
and colors, arranged
in a certain way on
the surface, with
the task of following
or transcribing
– not "representing" –
the flow of emotions.
"The first colors
that made a strong
impression on me,"
wrote Kandinsky
in *A Look at the Past*,
one of his many
theoretical essays,
"were light, vivid
green, white, scarlet,
black, and ochre ...
I saw these colors in
various objects,
which do not stand
before my eyes as
clearly today as the
colors themselves ..."
Objects and one's
perception of them,
therefore, may
become vague;
but not colors, whose
symbolic meaning
remains and actually
increases. Following
Kandinsky's example,
many painters and
sculptors tried
to elaborate on this
idea, relying
upon only
shape or color.

At the time that Chagall was working on *Peasant Life* (below), a number of artists in Europe were practicing abstract painting: their intention was not to represent what the eye sees, but rather to portray what the mind knows or imagines. In transcribing these images on to paper or canvas, it was necessary to organize them, either through the flow of free mental associations or according to an exact rational scheme. Kandinsky in Munich, and later Mondrian in the Netherlands, Brancusi in Romania, and Malevich in Russia, carried abstraction to its limits, striving for an absolute – "pure painting" – that would no longer be compromised by the natural appearance of things.

♦ **THE FIRST EXAMPLE**
Wassily Kandinsky,
*First Abstract
Watercolor*, 1910;
Paris, Nina
Kandinsky Collection.

Painted in Munich,
this first work in
which external reality
did not appear made a
huge impact upon
other painters.

9. CHAGALL'S LIFE ♦ *The "Free Academy" flourished, especially when, on Chagall's initiative, the sculpture, practical skills, and advertising sections were opened. Chagall was popular with his students, but relationships with his colleagues went less smoothly. Jealousy and misunderstandings arose, especially with Malevich, although he was a friend whose work Chagall greatly respected. Once, in Chagall's absence, Malevich took control of the academy and changed its name to the "Suprematist Academy". On his return, Chagall had Malevich arrested and was restored as director himself, but in 1920 he gave up and left Vitebsk for Moscow.* ➤

DIFFERENCES ♦
Above:
Marc Chagall,
Peasant Life,
1917-19; Private
collection.
Right:
Constantin Brancusi,
Endless Column,
1937; Tirgu Jiu,
Romania, public
gardens.

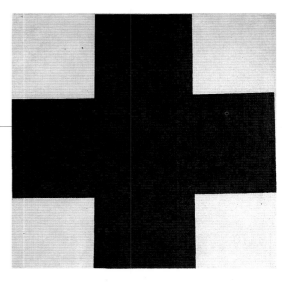

♦ ABSOLUTELY ABSTRACT
Kazimir Malevich, *Black Circle, Black Square,* and *Black Cross,* c.1923; St. Petersburg, Russian Museum.

In 1915, Kazimir Malevich drafted the manifesto of his Suprematist movement and painted the famous *Black Square on a White Ground.* Some time in the 1920s, he created the series of black geometrical figures shown here. With this, his idea of a painting of the absolute – and of an absolute that could be attained only through the absence of any recognizable objects – reached its ultimate state and became a mystical quest. Malevich had taken abstract painting even further than painters such as Kandinsky or Mondrian: instead of color and rhythm, there was only pure geometry and black, signifying the absence of color.

♦ METHODICAL
Piet Mondrian, *Red Tree,* 1908; *Blue Tree,* 1909-10; *Gray Tree;* and *Blossoming Apple Tree,* 1912; The Hague, Gemeentemuseum. In the Netherlands, Piet Mondrian moved toward abstract painting. In this tree series, which was the result of several years' work, he started from a basic representation of the tree, and slowly divested it of all naturalistic features (leaves, branches, landscape) until just its essential structure was left, seen as if through a mist. Having replaced the naturalistic elements with a few simple shapes – vertical and horizontal lines and curves – he eliminated these, in order to arrive at the tree's very soul. It can be said that Mondrian, like Malevich, was searching for the essence of things and tried to reach it by going beyond appearances. Like Malevich, he regarded abstract painting as a kind of revelation, a mystical vision, a bridge to the absolute, which could only be reached by the most rigorous simplicification and application of a method.

JEWISH THEATER

In 1920 Chagall created a series of paintings for the auditorium of Moscow's Jewish Theater. It was his first experience of interior decoration and the formula he used would be developed later for his great decorative works of the 1960s and '70s. His paintings in the theater are allegorical scenes. The *Introduction to the Jewish Theater* shows a kind of procession in which Chagall appears himself, carried in the arms of the art critic and patron Abram Efros. Music, Dance, Drama, and Literature are presented in four large panels. The frieze portrays a wedding banquet. Chagall's work turned the auditorium into a magic box where theater and painting, actors and audience, all became one.

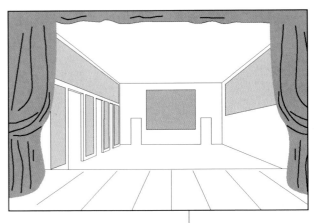

♦ NAMES
The characters look like saints, provided with "auras" in which Chagall wrote their names.

♦ THE INTERIOR
Chagall's paintings for the Jewish Theater covered the side walls of the auditorium.

♦ CHAGALL AND THE THEATER
Chagall had worked in the theater, in St. Petersburg, before the Revolution. He painted scenes and designed costumes. On one occasion, for the play *To Die Happy*, directed by Nikolai Yevreinov, he had even arranged for the actors to have their faces colored green and their hands blue, like characters in his paintings. After the Revolution, in Vitebsk, he had sketched scenes and costumes for Gogol's *Inspector General*, which was produced by the Revolutionary Satire Theater. Renewed attention was paid to Jewish culture after the Revolution and, in this climate, Chagall was charged with decorating the auditorium of the Jewish Theater in Moscow, which had been created from a large abandoned apartment. He drew his inspiration from typical Jewish and Russian traditions: ancient synagogues, whose multi-colored decorations made them look almost unreal; and the brightly painted interiors of peasant houses. Chagall's murals for the theater reflected the same concept of "total art" as Diaghilev tried to achieve with the Ballets Russes. All distinctions between painting, sculpture, music, and dance were abolished.

Above: the Jewish Theater in Moscow.

10. CHAGALL'S LIFE ♦ *Chagall arrived in Moscow, which was now the capital of the new U.S.S.R. He remained in dispute with the Ministry of Culture over the Vitebsk Academy and his departure from it, but meanwhile had been invited to take part in the first national exhibition of revolutionary art, where two rooms were assigned to him. The government purchased several of his works, although at a very low price. Abram Efros, the critic who had published the first monograph on Chagall's work, and Alexei Granovsky, the stage director, asked him to decorate the auditorium of the Jewish Theater. Enthusiastically, he completed the work in just forty days.* ⟫→

♦ PROCESSION
Marc Chagall, *Introduction to the Jewish Theater*, panel for the left wall of the theater, 1920; Moscow, Tretyakov Gallery. Chagall portrayed himself in the arms of the art critic Abram Efros, in the same way as icon painters represented the young Jesus being presented in the Temple.

With palette in hand, the painter is introduced to the mysteries of the Jewish Theater; next, the director Granovsky practices a dance step. A dwarf with a glass welcomes the guests according to gypsy ritual, while an orchestra of *klezmer* (musicians) behind him celebrate the wedding loudly.

♦ **THE FOUR ARTS**
Marc Chagall, *Music, Dance, Literature, Drama*, four panels for the right wall of the Jewish Theater, 1920; Moscow, Tretyakov Gallery. Chagall represented the arts as four allegorical figures. For the figure of Music, he clearly drew on the theme of his painting *The Violinist*.

♦ **GRANOVSKY ENTHRONED**
The entry point for the procession is in the background. At this side of the painting Granovsky sits motionless on a stool, as if on a throne. He is portrayed at the head of the procession too: as stage director and soul of the theater, he is present at the beginning and the end. Here, the upper part of his body, with the head as rigid as a statue's, has a regal air. It contrasts sharply with the lower part: Granovsky is bathing his feet in a basin. Chagall was representing both the cultivated and the popular side of the director's role.

♦ **UPROAR**
In the middle of the scene is a disc, which looks like a giant gramophone record. A fiddler-clown with his head detached is playing in the center of it. Around him, under the watchful gaze of a goat, is a bizarre orchestra of musicians and dancers. Some acrobats are leaving the orchestra, walking on their hands toward a kind of throne.

♦ **A LIKENESS**
A detail of the violin player from the *Introduction to the Jewish Theater*. The door by the violinist recalls the door in Chagall's 1917 painting *The Cemetery Gates,* which expressed the Jewish people's suffering and belief in their redemption.

A NEW PAINTER

Wide-open windows, broad views of the countryside, vases of flowers, and portraits of his wife Bella and their daughter Ida: Chagall's paintings after his return to Paris in 1923 were of the same subjects as the many evocative works he created in Russia in 1914-20, but the style had changed once again. The colors now blended, to convey a feeling of the light falling onto the scene. Chagall had set aside pictures that expressed some deeper meaning, and was basking in the pleasure of color; he began to paint landscapes, no longer as backgrounds but as the principal subjects of his works. He thus "turned French" in a way, linking himself to the great Impressionist tradition.

♦ RESTING
Marc Chagall, *The Poet Reclining*, 1915; London, The Tate Gallery.

♦ BELLA WITH FLOWERS
Marc Chagall, *Bella in Mourillon*, 1926; Paris, Ida Chagall Archives. In Mourillon, where he withdrew to paint, Chagall created many portraits of his wife, as well as landscapes and flower pictures.

♦ COMPARISON
Marc Chagall, *Lilies of the Valley*, 1916; Moscow, Tretyakov Gallery. In works like this from the Vitebsk years, objects are more sharply defined than in the later paintings.

♦ FANTASY
Marc Chagall, *Lovers in the Lilacs*, 1930; New York, private collection. Sometimes, in these years, landscapes and portraits merged together in astonishing inventions. Here, a giant vase of flowers, high up above a river, becomes a forest housing the two lovers, like a garden of Eden.

VARIATIONS ✦
Marc Chagall, *Ida at the Window*, 1924 (whole, below, and detail, right); Amsterdam, Stedelijk Museum. The scene is the same as in the painting *Window* (left): an open window, the countryside, and the sea in the background. Chagall represented it many times, as if to thoroughly investigate all of its pictorial possibilities. This time, he added the portrait of his daughter Ida and a vase of flowers.

✦ VIEW
Marc Chagall, *Window*, 1924; Zurich, Kunsthaus. Painted on the Ile de Bréhat, this is an example of Chagall's new painting style. The blue of the sea, the green of the countryside, and the gray of the window sill are reflected in the window panes.

A RECURRENT ✦ THEME
Marc Chagall, *Window in Zaolcha*, 1915; Moscow, Tretyakov Gallery. Two people in profile (Chagall and almost certainly Bella) are looking out of the window at the thick scrub surrounding the house. The astonished expressions on the faces and the shadowy landscape create a magical atmosphere.

11. CHAGALL'S LIFE ✦ *In 1922 Chagall left Russia for good. He went first to Berlin, where he found that many of the paintings left at the* Der Sturm *gallery in 1914 had been destroyed during the war. On September 1, 1923, he arrived in Paris. After several weeks, he was joined by Bella and Ida, and the family found lodgings in a damp room at the Hotel Médical in the Faubourg St. Jacques. Chagall set about repainting some of the lost works, perhaps to have his native Vitebsk close to him again; then, on the invitation of his painter friend Robert Delaunay and his wife Sonia, he began visiting the countryside. He moved for a while to a rented house in Brittany, on the Ile de Bréhat; the countryside became a more frequent central theme of his new paintings.* ⋙✦

AMBROISE VOLLARD

In 1923 the Paris art dealer Ambroise Vollard commissioned Chagall to illustrate the 19th-century novel *Dead Souls*, by the Russian writer Gogol. A successful result was virtually guaranteed, since Chagall's background matched the novel's rural and provincial setting. Vollard's next commission caused more controversy: he asked Chagall to illustrate La Fontaine's *Fables*. Some people doubted whether a foreigner could properly understand and interpret this great French classic. However, Vollard knew that the fables derived from Indian, Persian, Arab, and Chinese sources, and believed that Chagall had the visionary sensitivity to capture them vividly. Vollard also asked Chagall to produce some studies on the theme of the circus. The two men became good friends.

♦ THE DEALER
Ambroise Vollard (1865-1939) was one of the great dealers and promoters of new art during the late 19th century and the first decades of the 20th. He was a strong supporter of the Impressionist painters, but always showed an unfailing understanding of new trends.
He was a friend of Degas, Renoir, and Pissarro, and ardently promoted the work of Cézanne, setting up the first exhibition of the still-unknown painter's work at his gallery in the rue Lafitte in 1895.
He often went against the tide, and some of his initiatives became legendary: having bought a large part of the collection of Julien Tanguy (a canvas and paint merchant who accepted works by his Impressionist friends as payment for his goods), Vollard wrote to the artist Gauguin, who had moved to Tahiti, to offer himself as agent for all his works. Pablo Picasso and the Douanier Rousseau were also among the artists he supported. Vollard was the first to commission artists to illustrate literary classics and contemporary works. In this way, Chagall and others were introduced to a wider public.

Above:
Paul Cézanne,
Portrait of Ambroise Vollard, 1899;
Paris,
Musée du Petit Palais.

♦ THE CIRCUS
Marc Chagall, *The Acrobat*, 1930; Paris, Musée National d'Art Moderne. This work is one of the most charming of Chagall's paintings on circus subjects. The face descending from the sky to brush against the acrobat's cheek brings to mind the flying figures in such earlier paintings as *Over Vitebsk*.

♦ ON HORSEBACK
Marc Chagall, *The Beautiful Circus Rider*, 1930; London, Christie's. In the years following his return to Paris in 1923, Chagall produced many paintings, studies, and drawings of circus subjects. In this case, the circus rider resembles Bella. The clowns and animals are reminiscent of the fantastic creatures in earlier paintings.

♦ ACROBATICS
One of 19 preliminary gouaches on cardboard that Chagall painted for Vollard, 1927; Paris, Musée d'Art Moderne de la Ville. To distinguish the works in this series from others on the same subject, the two friends called them *The Vollard Circus*. Here, man and animal contemplate each other curiously.

♦ MEMORIES
OF RUSSIA
After Vollard's death in 1939, many of the illustrations he had commissioned Chagall to produce were published by Tériade. In these etchings for Gogol's *Dead Souls*, the character of Chichikov, a practiced swindler who cheated landowners in Russia, is portrayed as a grotesque giant, in effect a symbol of his country.
Left: *Chichikov at Pliushkin's*;
and right: *Pliushkin's Room*, 1924-25;
Moscow, Tretyakov Gallery.

1

2

3

♦ LA FONTAINE'S FABLES
Marc Chagall, illustrations for La Fontaine's *Fables*:
1) *The Donkey Loaded with Sponges and the Donkey*

Loaded with Salt;
2) *The Wolf, the Goat, and the Kid*;
3) *The Laughing Man and the Fish*;
4) *The Donkey and the Dog*;
5) *The Crow and the*

Fox; Paris, Musée National d'Art Moderne.
In 1927 Chagall exhibited the preliminary gouches for his etchings of La Fontaine's *Fables* at

the Bernheim-Jeune Gallery in Paris. Although the exhibition was not particularly successful, he decided to continue to produce the 100

planned illustrations, and this took him until 1930. The final illustrations are astonishing, both in style and from a technical point of view. Chagall had

combined several etching techniques and was perhaps the only artist who could have matched the variety of the *Fables* with a similar variety of illustrations.

4

5

12. CHAGALL'S LIFE ♦ *The years from 1923 to 1930, which Chagall spent either in Paris or in the countryside, were among the happiest he knew. He had become a famous and influential artist. Increasingly, Russian artists and stage directors sought him out to decorate an exhibition room or a theater. In 1923, he was commissioned by Ambroise Vollard to illustrate Gogol's* Dead Souls. *His friendship with Vollard, who came to his studio every day to take him to the circus or for a walk in the Bois de Boulogne, helped Chagall to broaden his contacts; he met artists including Vlaminck, Rouault, Maillol, and Picasso, and publishers such as Zervos and Tériade. Chagall and Bella could now live in comfort and led a more outgoing life: Diaghilev kept a box at their disposal at his Ballets Russes.* ⇒

THE BIBLE

After the illustrations for Gogol and La Fontaine, Vollard had another idea: to have Chagall illustrate nothing less than the Bible. It was an undertaking that no artist since Rembrandt had attempted. Generally, modern painters shied away from the idea of illustration, but Chagall was a unique personality in the 20th-century art world and Vollard felt that he was perhaps the only one who could accomplish such an undertaking. Moreover, the Bible had been part of Chagall's life since childhood. It was important to his religious life and a source of inspiration to him as an artist. In his etchings, he gave life to the Bible stories in a way that seemed to bring them closer to his own time. The patriarchs, kings, and prophets became real characters, and their stories became ordinary, everyday stories, while still retaining their miraculous character.

1

4

7

♦ **BOOKS OF THE BIBLE**
The word Bible, from the Greek biblia, simply means books. The Christian Bible is a collection of books, divided into two parts: the Old and the New Testaments. The Old Testament consists of 39 books (or 46 in the Catholic Bible), and the New Testament comprises the four Gospels (of Matthew, Mark, Luke, and John), which recount the story of Jesus, the Acts of the Apostles, the Letters, and the Book of Revelation. The Jewish Bible (called the *Tenakh*) is almost the same as the Christian Old Testament, but the books are arranged in a different order. In the Jewish Bible, the first five books comprise the Law (the Torah); the next twenty-one are the Prophets; and the last thirteen make up the Writings, which include the Psalms, the Proverbs, the Song of Songs, and Ecclesiastes. As for all Jews, the Bible was very important to Chagall. "I did not see the Bible, I dreamed of it," he said. Above and below: details from Chagall's illustration *Joseph Stripped by His Brothers,* 1931-39; Nice, Musée National Message Biblique.

♦ **THE MESSAGE**
Marc Chagall, *The Rainbow, a Sign of the Alliance between God and Men*, 1952; Nice, Musée National Message Biblique. All the etchings were a straightforward representation of the episodes from the Bible that Chagall had chosen. He added no personal interpretations. He believed that the biblical events would speak for themselves, through his illustrations, to convey their deep religious message.

2

3

♦ **CHAGALL'S BIBLE**
Marc Chagall, Illustrations of the Bible, 1931-39; Nice, Musée National Message Biblique.
1) *God Creates Man and Gives Him Life*;
2) *Jacob Struggling with the Angel*;
3) *Lot and His Daughters*;
4) *God Reveals Himself to Moses*;
5) *Joseph Stripped by His Brothers*;
6) *Abraham's Sacrifice*;
7) *Noah Releases the Dove*;
8) *Moses Causes Darkness to Fall upon Egypt*.

Chagall began work on his illustrations to the Bible in 1931, for Ambroise Vollard. Vollard's death in 1939, and then the Second World War, caused the artist to set aside the project for a long while, but in 1952 he was commissioned to continue and complete the work by the publisher Tériade. The illustrations were finished in 1956 and the Bible, including 115 etchings, was published by Tériade in 1957.

Chagall chose the episodes to illustrate, based on his own attitude rather than their traditional religious significance. He used the same method of working as when he had produced his previous illustrations: he began by painting a series of gouaches, from which he then worked to create the etchings. He tried to obtain, with the etching needle and acid, the same effects of light and shade as he had achieved, in the gouaches, with paint.

5

8

6

13. CHAGALL'S LIFE ♦ *In 1930 Vollard commissioned Chagall to illustrate the Bible. Before he began, Chagall wanted to acquaint himself with the places described in the Bible stories and so, in January 1931, he and Bella and Ida sailed for Palestine. They traveled through Egypt, visiting Alexandria and Cairo. In Palestine, they went to Haifa, Tel Aviv, and Jerusalem. To celebrate Chagall's arrival, Dizengoff, the mayor of Tel Aviv, met the artist surrounded by his firemen, who were the only uniformed personnel at his disposal. Chagall worked for some time in Tel Aviv, filling notebooks with drawings. He was impressed by the light that bathed the landscape: he said it seemed familiar, even though he was seeing it for the first time.* ⟫⁺

THE LOVERS AT THE EIFFEL TOWER

A young bride and groom rise in flight, supported by a giant bird. They are surrounded by musicians, angels, and festive images. From the time Chagall first saw Paris in 1910, the buildings and other landmarks of the French capital, from Notre-Dame to the quays by the Seine, made frequent appearances in his paintings. He would contrast them, sometimes very sharply, with the world of Vitebsk and his beloved repertoire of elderly Jews with the Torah, flying goats, angels, and lighted candles. In this painting, the wedding seems to concern not only the young couple – clearly Chagall and Bella – in their ceremonial finery, but also their two cities: Vitebsk, at the foot of the tree, and Paris, symbolized by the Eiffel Tower.

✦ **THE WORK**
The Lovers at the Eiffel Tower, 1938-39; oil on canvas, 148 x 145 cm. (58.5 x 57 in.); Paris, Musée National d'Art Moderne.
Painted while the artist was working on the Bible etchings, *The Lovers*, which forms one link in a long chain of Paris and Vitebsk views, is especially indicative of Chagall's happy mood at this time. He had purchased a beautiful house (the Villa Montmorency) in an elegant residential area near the Porte d'Auteuil. He met regularly with poets and philosophers such as Paul Eluard and René Schwob, the author of *Chagall and the Jewish Soul*, who acted as an intermediary between the painter and the philosopher Jacques Maritain. According to many experts on Chagall's work, the characteristic painting style of those years – free-flowing, often playing with soft variations of the same color – was a result of his contact with poetry and with philosophy.

Above and below: two details of the canvas.

✦ **REAL AND REMEMBERED**
Marc Chagall, *Self-Portrait with Seven Fingers*, 1912-13 (detail); Amsterdam, Stedelijk Museum.

Paris, with the Eiffel Tower, is presented as seen through the window; Vitebsk, in the painting on the easel, as remembered in the artist's heart.

✦ **A DREAM**
Marc Chagall, *Self-Portrait*, 1958-59 (detail); Florence, Uffizi. In Chagall's later paintings, Paris, represented by its famous buildings such as Notre-Dame, sometimes appears as a dream.

The painting, dominated by the dark blue vertical of the Eiffel Tower, is an allegory of earthly happiness: an ode to marital love and universal harmony. The use of the same light, cool tones across the whole picture, culminating in the white of the bride's wedding gown, has the effect of unifying all the varied scenes and subjects portrayed. The large, cheerful bird became another element in Chagall's repertoire of images.

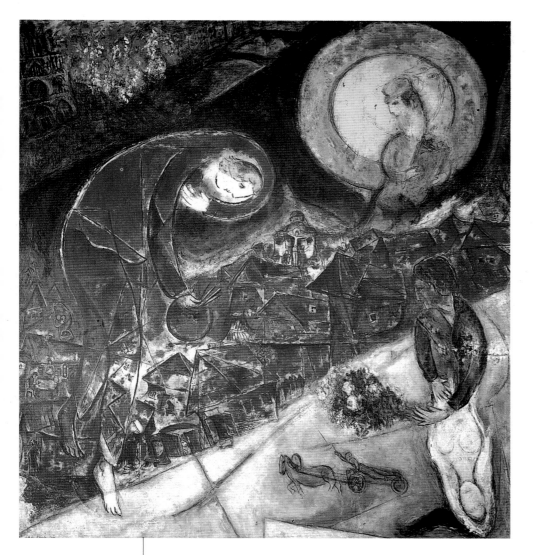

DETAILS ✦
Two mysterious details from *Red Roofs*. Above: a horse-drawn cart makes its way toward the two cities. Right: the figure of a bride forms the lower part of the figure of a man with a bouquet. It is likely that Chagall wanted the figure to represent himself as a young man, with Bella, in her wedding gown, as part of him.

✦ **TWO CITIES**
Marc Chagall, *Red Roofs*, 1953-54; Paris, private collection. Chagall portrays himself bowing reverently before a man with a Torah scroll, and also before his beloved cities: Vitebsk, with its red roofs, and Paris, symbolized by Notre-Dame (top left).

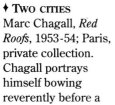

✦ **PARIS**
Marc Chagall, *Paris from the Window*, 1913; New York, Solomon R. Guggenheim Museum. This magnificent view of Paris was painted during the same period as the *Self-Portrait with Seven Fingers*. Here, the French capital is portrayed as a source of wonders – a cat with a human face, a two-headed man, an upside-down train, a parachutist, and, above all, the towering silhouette of the Eiffel Tower.

✦ **FLOWERS**
A detail from *Paris from the Window*. Flowers in the foreground, against a view, became a recurring motif in Chagall's later paintings. The bouquet on a chair in *Paris from the Window* was the first example.

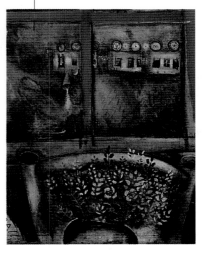

SURREALISM

Impossible and incongruous situations and man-animal figures appeared frequently in Chagall's paintings, which therefore seemed to have some affinity with the new Surrealist movement. In literature, film, and art, the Surrealists sought to release the unconscious forces that civilization had repressed. To do so, they used various techniques, from automatic writing and dream-recall to provocative public gestures. For several years, their belief in personal liberation led the Surrealists to subscribe to the ideas of the revolutionary left, but Surrealism and disciplined political action proved irreconcilable, and disillusion soon set in.

♦ **METAMORPHOSIS**
Paul Delvaux, *Aurora*, 1937; Venice, Peggy Guggenheim Collection.

Amid mysterious architecture, the light of the rising sun turns the tree trunks into women.

♦ **MAN-ANIMAL**
Marc Chagall, *A Midsummer Night's Dream*, 1939; Grenoble, Musée de Peinture.
In this work, inspired by Shakespeare's comedy, a man with a donkey's head embraces the young bride, while a winged figure flies across the sky.

♦ **SURREALIST VISION**
Salvador Dalì, *Premonition of Civil War* or *Soft Construction with Boiled Beans*, 1936; Philadelphia, Museum of Art. Dalì's paintings often portray apocalyptic scenes, as if to proclaim the end of the world.

♦ **SURREALIST STREET**
One of the gallery's long corridors was turned into the *rue Surréaliste* (Surrealist Street), by installing twenty mannequins in provocative, ironic, or absurd poses. Stree signs were hung above them, with absurd or funny imaginary names, such as "Blood Transfusion Street".

♦ THE EXHIBITION
On January 7, 1938, the Exposition Internationale du Surréalisme opened at the Galerie des Beaux-Arts in Paris. It attracted many curious visitors.

IRONIC ♦
René Magritte, *The Treason of Images*, 1928-29; Los Angeles, County Museum of Art. "This is not a pipe," the writing below the image warns: perhaps because it is only a picture of one?

♦ MYSTERIOUS
René Magritte, *The Voice of Air*, 1942; Venice, Peggy Guggenheim Collection.

♦ THE MAGIC CAVERN
Marcel Duchamp turned the exhibition's central room into a kind of cave of wonders, by hanging 1,200 bags of coal from the ceiling.

♦ OUT OF TIME
Max Ernst, *The Robing of the Bride*, 1939-40; Venice, Peggy Guggenheim Collection.
In a magic-laden atmosphere, mysterious figures and feathered warriors engage in a strange ceremony.

♦ WATER TAXI
At the exhibition's entrance, Salvador Dalì placed his *Taxi pluvieux* (Rainy Taxi), a real taxi with two mannequins inside that were constantly hit by jets of water.

THE WHITE CRUCIFIXION

A beam of light floods down over the large white crucifix standing in the middle of the canvas. The figure of Christ is not clothed in the usual loin-cloth but in a traditional Jewish prayer shawl. Around him, also in white light, are pictures of a world that seems to have gone mad: burning houses, soldiers marching, an elderly Jew fleeing, a mother carrying her baby away in her arms, rabbis in despair. Chagall's usual motifs are repeated here, but the atmosphere has changed into one of immense tragedy. Chagall created this work at a time when Jews and others were suffering persecution by the Nazis and Europe was on the brink of war.

♦ **MOTHER AND CHILD** A detail from the bottom right of *The White Crucifixion*. The frightened-looking woman running away from the fire, with her baby in her arms, seems almost to be stepping out of the canvas.

♦ **THE WORK**
Marc Chagall, *The White Crucifixion*, 1938; oil on canvas, 155 x 140 cm. (61 x 55 in.); Chicago, The Art Institute. Chagall began this large painting in 1937, at the time when he was working on the Bible etchings. More and more reports were reaching France about persecutions of Jews by the Nazi regime in Hitler's Germany. Some of Chagall's paintings had been publicly burned in Germany as examples of "degenerate art", and as a Jew he would be in danger if war came. He swung between moments of utter gloom and rare intervals when he could still manage to create cheerful images. However, anti-semitism was seeping out of Germany and even infecting some French people. Chagall, who had rejoiced at the end of discrimination against Jews at the time of the Russian Revolution, felt as if history was turning full circle.

Above and below: two details from *The White Crucifixion*.

♦ **THE SYNAGOGUE**
Fire that destroys and forces people to flee is a recurring theme in Chagall's painting. Perhaps the tales he had heard from his family about the fire in Vitebsk on the day he was born were one source of the theme. In this detail from *The White Crucifix*, the reference is to the Nazis, who were setting fire to synagogues in Germany.

The white and gray tones of this painting, combined with its scenes of terror and destruction, create its unique atmosphere. The crucified Jesus is the still center, surrounded by a frantic and terrible energy. By covering him with a prayer shawl, Chagall emphasizes Jesus's Jewishness; but the exact meaning of the work is debatable. Is Chagall making a comparison between the persecution and murder of Jews and the crucifixion of Christ?

♦ GRIEF AND FLIGHT

Above: in this detail from *The White Crucifixion*, three rabbis and a woman, hovering like frightened birds, cover their eyes, so as not to see, or make gestures of despair. Left: an elderly Jew in a cap, and with a sack slung over his shoulder, flees through the flames that are consuming the abandoned Torah scroll.

♦ A 16TH-CENTURY EXAMPLE

In Italy in 1937, Chagall had studied several crucifixions of the Venetian school. This large fresco by Pordenone, painted in 1520 in the cathedral of Cremona, gives an idea of the examples he may have had in mind when painting *The White Crucifixion*.

♦ REFUGEES

Some exhausted refugees lean from a drifting boat, while others wave their arms for help. Every detail in the painting adds to the atmosphere of despair.

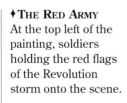

♦ A FLEEING JEW

The Jew running away in the left foreground seems to be trying to move a scroll to safety.

♦ THE RED ARMY

At the top left of the painting, soldiers holding the red flags of the Revolution storm onto the scene.

♦ COMPARISON

Marc Chagall, *Golgotha,* 1912 (detail); New York, MOMA. Chagall painted this work when under the influence of Cubist geometry and his friend Delaunay's Orphism. However, there are similarities between *Golgotha* and *The White Crucifixion*, in the use of a single dominant color and in the device of isolating the figure of Christ on the cross in a beam of light.

NEW YORK

In the early 1940s many artists fleeing war-torn
Europe went to live in New York. The arrival of the
Surrealists, in particular, provided a powerful stimulus
for American artists, who for a long time had looked
to Europe, and especially Paris, as the pre-eminent
model. New York City was beginning to give birth to
artistic languages of its own, each very different from
the other. For example, the stock market crash of
1929 and the ensuing Great Depression gave rise
to the socially committed art of Isabel Bishop and
Edward Hopper. On the other hand, the art of
Arshile Gorky, Willem de Kooning, and Jackson
Pollock emphasized spontaneity. Their work gave
rise to the new technique of action painting and the
Abstract Expressionist idiom that dominated the
post-war period and made New York the new art
capital of the world.

♦ BISHOP
Isabel Bishop, *Virgil
and Dante in Union
Square*, 1932;
Wilmington, Delaware
Art Museum. Europe
and America combined.

♦ NOSTALGIA
Marc Chagall, *In My
Home*, 1943; Turin,
Modern Art Gallery.
In New York, Chagall
often painted ordinary
views of Vitebsk.

♦ GORKY
Arshile Gorky,
Untitled, 1944;
Venice, Peggy
Guggenheim
Collection.

Gorky spread his
colors freely,
following the
impulses of the hand,
as in the Surrealists'
"automatic writing".

♦ DE KOONING
Willem de Kooning,
Composition, 1958;
Venice, Peggy
Guggenheim

Collection. Like
Gorky's, de Kooning's
style was very free,
but he favored the
expressive gesture.

THE STUDIO ♦
One of the paintings
hung in Chagall's
New York studio was

To My Wife, a work
which he had begun
in 1933 and
completed in 1944.

EDWARD HOPPER ♦
Edward Hopper, *Night Hawks*, 1942; Chicago, The Art Institute. Many of Hopper's paintings seemed to express the loneliness of city life. However, he also painted country scenes in a different style.

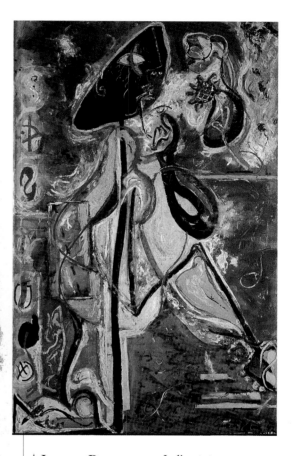

♦ **JACKSON POLLOCK**
Jackson Pollock, *Moon-Woman*, 1942; Venice, Peggy Guggenheim Collection. Traces of Indian totems can be seen in Pollock's works. Painting seemed like a magical ritual in which he immersed himself.

14. CHAGALL'S LIFE ♦ *In the 1930s Chagall traveled widely in Europe. When the Second World War began he took refuge briefly in southern France, but was then invited to New York by the Museum of Modern Art. He arrived there on June 23, 1940, the day after Russia was invaded by the Nazis and many cities, including Vitebsk, were set on fire. He took only two paintings with him:* The White Crucifixion *and* A Midsummer Night's Dream. *Anguished by events in Europe, he lived at first like a stranger. Since he knew no English, he spent most of his time with Jewish craftsmen in Manhattan, with whom he spoke Yiddish, the language of East European Jews. In 1943, at the insistence of Léonide Massine, an acclaimed Russian choreographer, Chagall painted the sets for a performance at the New York Ballet Theater of a ballet by Tchaikovsky.* ➸

BELLA'S DEATH

Of the many paintings that Chagall dedicated to his wife's death, the first ones – *Around Her* and *The Wedding Candles* – are also the best examples of his astonishing ability to adapt the usual repertoire of images to ever-changing expressive needs. The circus, the acrobats, the lighted candles, and even the views of Vitebsk suddenly shift their mood, as if under a spell; the atmosphere around them changes and, instead of joy, they now express deep grief over Bella's death. The same happens in the painting *The Soul of the City*, where another familiar subject – the artist at his easel – becomes a pretext to call up memories of his beloved wife.

♦ TWO WORKS, ONE SUBJECT
Chagall began to work on *Around Her* and *The Wedding Candles* in the spring of 1945. In his studio he found a large canvas, 2.5 m. (8 ft. 2 in.) wide and 1.2 m. (3ft. 11 in.) high, on which he had previously painted a circus scene entitled *The Harlequins*. In the center of the scene was a half-figure of Bella dressed in party clothes. A flying acrobat was about to present her with a crystal ball on which a view of Vitebsk had been painted. On the right-hand side of the painting, a wedding procession was entering the circus world, and being welcomed by the usual band of jubilant characters. Chagall now divided this canvas into two parts and painted over his previous work to create the two new paintings. *Around Her* became an emotional remembrance, in which the crystal ball with the Vitebsk view glitters in the deep blue, beyond the clouds.
In *The Wedding Candles*, Chagall retained the bride and groom and the goat-headed figure from his original painting, but everything else was changed. A train of ghosts follows the bridal couple and the blue angel, once an acrobat, appears to announce only mournful events.

Above: a detail from *Around Her.*

15. CHAGALL'S LIFE ♦ *Bella died on September 2, 1944, in the country house at Cranberry Lake, north of New York City, where Chagall had retired to paint. Her death was sudden, caused by a seemingly harmless viral infection. The terrible loss struck the artist just when good news was coming from Europe: Paris had been liberated from the Germans, the war was coming to an end, and he would soon be able to return. In the months preceding her death, Bella had completed her memoirs,* Burning Lights *and* First Encounter. ➤

♦ LAMENT IN GRAY
Marc Chagall, *The Soul of the City*, 1945; Paris, Musée National d'Art Moderne.
In this painting Bella. reappears like a ghost next to the painter, who is shown with two faces.

♦ LIGHT
In this detail from *Around Her,* a bird flies into the picture, holding a lighted candle in its hand-like claws. Against the blue, the candle flame seems to illuminate the entire scene.

♦ REMEMBRANCE
Marc Chagall, *Around Her*, 1945; Paris, Musée National d'Art Moderne.
Deep emotion animates the whirl of figures around the crystal ball and Bella, on the right, who seems to be weeping.

♦ UPSIDE-DOWN
A detail from *Around Her*. Chagall portrays himself at his easel with his head upside-down, in the same way as in a drawing made in 1918 (see page 10). In the painting, the upside-down head may symbolize a total capsizing of the artist's world, putting in doubt all his cherished convictions.

TWO FACES ♦
A detail from *The Soul of the City*. Again Chagall portrays himself at the easel, this time painting a crucifixion. Here he gives himself two faces, one looking at the canvas, the other at the ghostly apparition of Bella. The dominant color of the painting is a deep and mournful gray.

♦ BELLA
Bella is portrayed with an asbent air. In *Around Her* (detail, below), she touches her hand to her face as though she is weeping.
In *The Soul of the City* (detail, bottom) she is white and flying like a ghost.

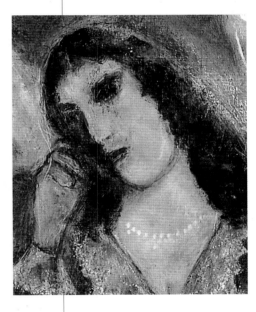

♦ FUNERAL PROCESSION
Marc Chagall, *The Wedding Candles*, 1945; Paris, private collection.
Chagall painted this on top of the right-hand part of an earlier work, in which the newly-weds were entering a colorful circus world.

He darkened what had been a festive scene with blue, giving a feeling of mourning. The two lovers leaning on a giant bird here express melancholy, whereas in earlier works, such as *The Lovers at the Eiffel Tower*, they were a symbol of joy.

THE FLAYED OX

At night, a skinned and disemboweled ox hangs from a pole in the center of a village square covered with snow. The ox shape has a resemblance to a crucifix, the hind legs suggesting arms. It is red from the blood that is dripping into a wooden trough below. A rooster is running away terrified from this image of death, and another is perched on a roof top. The familiar figure of an elderly Jew flies in from above, rending the black of the night: his face is green and he is holding a bloody knife. Curving over him is a lighted candle which seems to be going out. Below, the faces of a peasant woman and bearded man emerge from one of the roofs. The woman stares at the incomprehensible scene that is taking place only a few steps away.

Almost ten years
earlier, in 1938,
the horror of Nazi
persecutions of Jews
had inspired Chagall
to paint the dramatic
White Crucifixion.
The Flayed Ox,
another scene of
suffering, was
created after he
returned to Paris
from New York
in 1946.
It sums up
all of the tragedies
that had occurred in
his life since 1938:
the terrible effects of
the war, the burning
and destruction of
Vitebsk, and the
death of Bella.
Chagall had painted a
skinned ox before, in
1929. However, that
had been less
emotionally fraught.
He had even included
a vase of flowers next
to the carcass and
shown it opposite a
bright landscape.
The subject of the
slaughtered ox was
also connected in
Chagall's mind with
memories of Vitebsk
and his years at La
Ruche in Paris (see
page 16).
Above and below:
two details of
The Flayed Ox.

♦ **DESPAIR**
A figure with a clock
face hangs out of the
window. This detail
of the painting may
symbolize the end
of time after so
much horror.

♦ **DETAILS**
The painting is
crowded with
apparently symbolic
details, such as the
green-faced, wide-
eyed elderly Jew
(above) and the knife
he is holding, the
bent-over candle that
is burning out, and
the two frightened
roosters, one on a
roof, the other in the
street (below).
Chagall's intention
was not to describe
an actual event but to
create an atmosphere
of tragedy and terror
with a universal
application.

Built on the sharp contrast between warm tones of bright red and cold tones of the landscape's white and blue, this painting has the dramatic power of a sudden scream. The subject of a skinned ox has been painted by many artists, from Rembrandt to Soutine. Chagall made the animal resemble the figure of Christ on the cross — perhaps an allusion to the suffering of the Jews in the war. As so often with Chagall's works, a single explanation is difficult to find for all the symbols that crowd the scene.

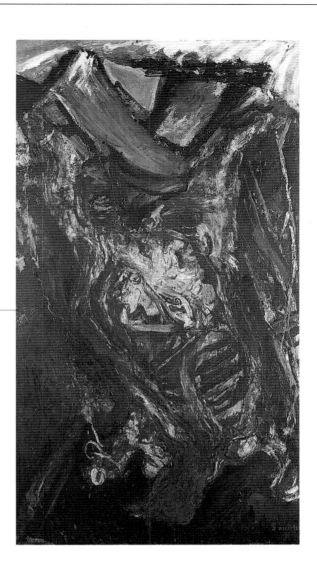

♦ **FRANCIS BACON**
Francis Bacon, *Painting*, 1946; New York, MOMA. The skinned ox was also taken as a subject by the British painter Francis Bacon, whose imagination created masterworks of horror and despair.

CHAIM SOUTINE ♦
Chaim Soutine, *Skinned Ox*, 1925; Grenoble, Musée de Peinture et de Sculpture. The volatile Russian painter Soutine was a friend of Chagall. They both had studios at La Ruche in Paris.

REMBRANDT ♦
Rembrandt van Rijn, *The Quartered Ox*, 1655; Paris, Louvre: probably the most famous quartered ox in the history of art, and one that all artists have looked to as a model.

♦ **MIRRORED**
Mario Mafai, *Quartered Ox*, 1930; Milan, Pinacoteca di Brera.

Contemporary with Chagall, the Italian painter Mario Mafai was part of an Expressionist group in Rome. He too was fascinated by the subject of the skinned ox, painting it double, as if in a mirror.

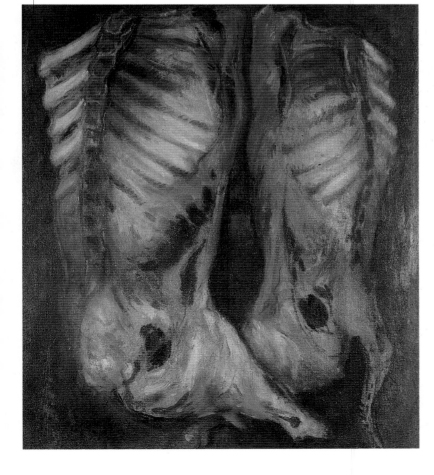

BRILLIANT INTERIORS

In the 1960s, André Malraux, a celebrated writer and France's Minister of Cultural Affairs, decided to arrange for the ceilings of some of the most famous theaters in Paris to be decorated. Among them were the Odéon and the Opéra. To work on the Odéon, Malraux chose the painter André Masson. For the Opéra, a great symbol of Second Empire Paris, he selected Chagall. For a long time the concept of integrating the visual arts with architecture had been honored, but it was only in the second half of the 20th century that artists were regularly employed on great public commissions. Chagall was a prime example, using a variety of techniques and working in several media in addition to paint, notably mosaic, stained glass, and tapestry.

♦ THE CEILING OF THE OPÉRA
Decorating the ceiling of the Opéra took two years (1962-64) and the finished work was recognized immediately as an extraordinary success. Chagall divided the large circular dome into five zones, each containing several scenes. The whole portrayed the Olympus of classical music. Tchaikovsky, Mussorgsky, Ravel, Wagner, and Mozart are present, with scenes from their most famous works: *Swan Lake, Boris Godunov, Daphne and Chloë, Tristan and Isolde, The Magic Flute.* The figures are set against a typical Paris panorama. For example, the detail above shows the Eiffel Tower and the one below, the Arc de Triomphe and the Place de la Concorde. The ceiling is one of the finest examples of the great decorative cycles that Chagall created in his mature years. In the same period, he also worked on stained glass windows for the synagogue in the Hadassah Medical Center in Jerusalem, and on interior decorations for the Lincoln Center in New York.

♦ ANGEL
The figure of a golden angel in flight, which appears in many of Chagall's paintings, returns in the Opéra ceiling, linking two scenes.

♦ PARIS LANDMARKS
Behind the scenes from operas and ballets, Chagall represented many famous Paris buildings. They include the Eiffel Tower, the Madeleine, the Obelisk in the Place de la Concorde, and the façade of the Opera house itself.

♦ CERAMICS

Marc Chagall, *Flowers*, ceramic plaque, 1951; Private collection. Chagall watched several potters at work in Vence, and tried his hand at ceramics too. He began by decorating rectangular and round plates, and went on to produce ceramic tiles, plaques, and vases.

THE OPÉRA ♦

Designed by the architect Charles Garnier, the Opéra was built in 1860-75. An incredible amount of precious marble had to be obtained from all of the main quarries in France.

THE ODÉON ♦

The ceiling of the Odéon National Theater, decorated by André Masson in 1965. Masson was closely connected with the Surrealist movement. He used the circular ceiling as a surface on which to paint abstract shapes.

♦ STAINED GLASS

In 1967-78, Chagall completed a series of twelve stained glass windows for an English country church, All Saints, in Tudeley, in the county of Kent. The work was commissioned by Lady d'Avigdor-Goldsmid in memory of her daughter. Chagall took his inspiration for the work from the theme of the Resurrection.

16. CHAGALL'S LIFE ♦ *A retrospective exhibition of Chagall's work opened in New York City in 1946, in which year the artist returned to Paris. Another exhibition opened in Paris in 1947, at the Musée d'Art Moderne. Chagall was now a celebrity, almost a living legend. In 1950, he moved to Vence, in the South of France, close to where Matisse and Picasso lived, and in 1952 he married Valentina Brodsky. New artistic undertakings now included stained glass windows, murals, mosaics, and ceramics. Chagall's output in these years was greater than ever. In 1967, the Soviet Minister of Culture invited him to Russia and in 1973, after a 50-year absence, he did return to Moscow. He refused to go to Vitebsk, however: the war had left scars that he had no wish to see.* ⇒♦

THE MUSEUM OF THE BIBLICAL MESSAGE

♦ DESIGNED FOR MEDITATION
As Chagall worked on his illustrations to the Bible, he conceived the idea of a building devoted to displaying a cycle of biblical paintings, conveying a "biblical message". Intending to use an ancient chapel – the Calvary Chapel – on the hills near Vence, he created 17 large canvases, of which 12 were inspired by Genesis and Exodus and 5 by the Song of Songs. However, the chapel turned out to be unsuitable for the project, and Chagall's friend André Malraux persuaded him to donate the paintings to the French state. This was in 1966; two years later, work began on the special museum in Nice. Other artists at this time had undertaken similar projects in and around Vence, in an attempt to establish a new relationship between art and architecture: Matisse had decorated the Rosary Chapel in Vence, Picasso, the chapel in Vallauris, and Cocteau, one in Villefranche. However, the only real equivalent of Chagall's Museum is in Houston, Texas, where Mark Rothko, another artist of Russian descent, created a chapel decorated with large, almost monochrome paintings – an invitation to silence and meditation.

Above:
Marc Chagall.

The National Museum of the Biblical Message in Nice is a unique place. It was the first museum ever to be devoted to a living artist and, more than just a museum, it is a religious building, inviting meditation and spiritual experience unconnected with any specific religious affiliation. Chagall's large paintings on biblical themes, the gouaches and etchings he created to illustrate the Bible, his mosaics, tapestries, and stained glass windows: all these together convey the artist's vision of a strange, troubled, yet deeply spiritual universe, filled with strife and beauty. Chagall's museum is a living, vital place, reflecting his belief in the living message of the Bible.

♦ MOSES
Marc Chagall, *Moses Receiving the Tablets of the Law*, 1956-58; Nice, Musée National Message Biblique. This illustrates Exodus 34, in which God gives Moses the Ten Commandments.

CONCERT HALL ♦
The building also has a concert hall, with stained glass windows on the theme of the creation of the world.

17. CHAGALL'S LIFE ♦ *Chagall's trip to Moscow in 1973 was marked by a retrospective exhibition of his work at the Tretyakov Gallery. On his return to France, the Marc Chagall National Museum of the Biblical Message was opened in Nice, on the artist's birthday, July 7. This was a consecration, but by no means marked the end, of Chagall's work. Indeed, he continued with renewed enthusiasm. The following year, his stained glass windows for Reims Cathedral were inaugurated, followed by those for The Art Institute in Chicago and those for Chichester Cathedral in England. Exhibitions of his work were held in many places, from Sweden to Japan. On March 28, 1985, Chagall died suddenly of a heart attack in his house in Vence. He was 97 years old.*

♦ **ABRAHAM**
Marc Chagall,
*Abraham and the
Three Angels*,
1956-58; Nice,
Musée National
Message Biblique.

♦ **THE OPENING**
The museum is
opened on
July 7, 1973, by
Chagall's friend and
former Minister of
Cultural Affairs
André Malraux.

GENESIS ♦
Marc Chagall,
The Creation of Man,
1956-58; Nice,
Musée National
Message Biblique.
The creation of
human life is
expressed by an
explosion of color.

♦ **THE MUSEUM**
The museum is
situated on a hill at
Cimiez, Nice, and is
surrounded by a
garden of pine,
cypress, and olive
trees. It houses works
by Marc Chagall that
he donated to the
French state.
Chagall created the
stained glass windows
for the concert hall in
the museum and also
the mosaic that
overlooks a pond
outside. The
atmosphere is
peaceful, to help
visitors appreciate the
spiritual message of
the works.

◆ KEY DATES IN CHAGALL'S LIFE

1887 — Moshe Zakharovich Shagal is born on July 7 in a suburb of Vitebsk, in Belarus. He is the first of nine children in a Hasidic Jewish family.

1907 — Having studied with Yehuda Pen in Vitebsk, Moshe goes to live in St. Petersburg, then capital of the Russian empire, to further his art training.

1910 — Moshe moves to Paris where he meets poets such as Apollinaire and Cendrars and painters such as Delaunay. He changes his name to Marc Chagall.

1914 — In Berlin, Chagall exhibits his works for the first time and even sells a few. He returns to Vitebsk, where he marries Bella Rosenfeld on July 25, 1915. The First World War has begun.

1916 — Chagall works in a government military office in St. Petersburg. His daughter Ida is born. In his paintings he focuses on subjects from everyday life.

1917 — The Russian Revolution overthrows the old regime. Like many artists during these unsettled times, Chagall tends to return to traditional artistic values.

1919 — The revolutionary government appoints Chagall director of a new art academy in Vitebsk – one of many created in Russia with the idea of using art to educate the people.

1920 — In the post-war years, new artistic trends develop, such as abstract painting. Chagall is in Moscow, where he creates paintings for the walls of the Jewish Theater.

1923 — Chagall returns to Paris, and begins to paint landscapes as the principal subjects of his works. He meets Vollard, who commissions him to illustrate Gogol's *Dead Souls*.

1927 — Vollard next commissions Chagall to illustrate La Fontaine's *Fables*. The Chagalls are experiencing a period of wealth and happiness.

1931 — Vollard commissions Chagall to illustrate the Bible. So that the artist can see the biblical sites before embarking on this project, the Chagalls visit Egypt and Palestine.

1933 — Hitler becomes Chancellor in Germany. In a few years Europe will again be plunged into war. Persecution of Jews begins to escalate.

1938 — The International Surrealist Exhibition opens in Paris. Chagall paints *The White Crucifixion*, perhaps comparing the suffering of Jesus with that of the Jews.

1939 — September 1: The invasion of Poland by German troops under Hitler's command sets off the Second World War. The Chagalls move to southern France.

1940 — The Metropolitan Museum of Modern Art invites Chagall to New York, refuge for many artists during the war. Chagall begins to paint theater and ballet scenery.

1944 — Bella dies in September, just when the war is nearing an end. *The Wedding Candles* and *Around Her,* 1945, are the first of many works that Chagall dedicates to her death.

1946 — Chagall returns to Paris, now a celebrity. In the 1950s, he moves to the South of France and marries Valentina Brodsky in 1952. Many new artistic undertakings begin.

1948 — The State of Israel, a safehaven for all Jewish survivors of the war, is founded on May 13. Chagall is invited there to create the stained glass windows for the synagogue in the Hadassah Medical Center in Jerusalem.

1967 — At the invitation of the Soviet Ministry of Culture, Chagall returns to Moscow, but refuses to visit Vitebsk, which has been altered beyond recognition by the war and the ensuing reconstruction.

1973 — The Museum of the Biblical Message is opened in Nice, France, on Chagall's birthday, July 7. It is the first museum ever to be devoted to a living artist. Chagall is still fully active.

1985 — Chagall dies of a sudden heart attack on March 28, in his French home of Saint-Paul-de-Vence, at the age of 97.

◆ WHERE TO SEE WORKS BY CHAGALL

Most of the many works that Chagall painted during his long life are to be found in the places where he lived. The majority of his work from the period 1914-22 is in museums and galleries in Russia. Art museums in France, where he chose to settle and whose culture he absorbed, hold a large part of his production. Also, many paintings are in galleries in the U.S.A., where Chagall lived during the Second World War. Some works are part of private collections, especially in the U.S.A., but also in France. Particularly significant are the Ida Chagall Archives, in both Paris and Basel, Switzerland. There is also the Marc Chagall Museum of the Biblical Message in Nice.

Of course, some of Chagall's works are to be seen in the places for which he created them: for example, the ceiling of the Paris Opera, the decorations for the Lincoln Center in New York, and the stained glass windows for the church of All Saints in Tudeley, England, and for the synagogue of the Hadassah Medical Center in Jerusalem.

Below is a list of the museums that hold the richest collections of Chagall's work. Private collections are not included.

FRANCE

NICE, MUSÉE NATIONAL MESSAGE BIBLIQUE MARC CHAGALL
The Museum of the Biblical Message was created by the artist himself and opened in 1973. Here are 17 large canvases inspired by the Bible, 39 temperas, 105 etchings, 75 lithographs, 5 sculptures, a ceramic piece, and a tapestry. Chagall also created stained glass windows for the concert hall in the museum, and a mosaic.

PARIS, MUSÉE NATIONAL D'ART MODERNE
This museum holds a very large collection of Chagall's works, including the 1907 *Self-Portrait, The Dead* (1908), the *Self-Portrait in Green* (1914), and works from the artist's early Paris years such as *To Russia, Asses, and Others* (1911-12), *The Newspaper Vendor* (1914), the *Double Portrait with Wineglass* (1917-18), *Bella with a White Collar* (1917), *The Acrobat* (1930), *The Lovers at the Eiffel Tower* (1938-39), *Around Her* (1945), *The Soul of the City* (1945), *The Fall of Icarus* (1975), and the illustrations created in the late 1920s. for La Fontaine's *Fables*.

RUSSIA

MOSCOW, TRETYAKOV GALLERY
The Tretyakov Gallery's Chagall collection is especially rich in works dating from the 1914-22 period, including *Over the Town* (1914-18), *My Uncle's Store in Lyozno* (1914), *View from the Window in Vitebsk* (1914-15), *Window in Zaolcha* (1915), *Lilies of the Valley* (1916), *War to the Palaces* (1918-19).

The Gallery also holds Chagall's illustrations for Gogol's *Dead Souls* and the paintings that the artist created for the walls of the Jewish Theater in Moscow in 1920: *Introduction to the Jewish Theater, Literature, Music, Dance, Drama.* These were only recently brought to light, having long been buried in the Gallery's basement.

ST. PETERSBURG, RUSSIAN STATE MUSEUM
This museum in the old capital of the Russian empire holds *The Red Jew* (1914-15), *The Mirror* (1915), and *The Promenade* (1917-18).

USA

NEW YORK, METROPOLITAN MUSEUM OF MODERN ART
Among other works by Chagall, the Metropolitan Museum holds *I and the Village* (1911), *Golgotha* (1912), *The Birthday* (1915), *The Cemetery Gates* (1917), *Over Vitebsk* (1915-20), and *Time is a River with No Banks* (1930-39).

NEW YORK, THE SOLOMON R. GUGGENHEIM MUSEUM
The collections of this museum include some important works by Chagall: *The Drinking Soldier* (1911-12), *Paris through the Window* (1913), and *The Green Violinist* (1923).

PHILADELPHIA, PHILADELPHIA MUSEUM OF ART
This museum holds *The Poet, or Half Past Three* (1911), *To My Fiancée* (1911), *Self-Portrait with White Collar* (1914), *The Wounded Soldier* (1914), and *The Water Tub* (1925).

HOLLAND

AMSTERDAM, STEDELIJK MUSEUM
Works by Chagall held by the Stedelijk Museum include *The Violinist* (1912-13), *Self-Portrait with Seven Fingers* (1912-13), *Pregnant Woman* (1913), *Ida at the Window* (1924), *Lovers with Half Moon* (1926-27), *The Acrobat* (1931), and *Madonna with Sleigh* (1947).

♦ LIST OF WORKS INCLUDED IN THIS BOOK

(A letter W after a page number indicates that the work concerned is reproduced whole. The letter D after a page number indicates that a detail of the work is shown.)

The works reproduced in this book are listed here, with (when known) their date, their dimensions, the place they are currently housed, and the page number. The numbers in bold type refer to the credits on page 64.
Abbreviations:
PGC = Peggy Guggenheim Collection, Venice
TGM = Tretyakov Gallery, Moscow
MNAM = Musée National d'Art Moderne, Paris
MOMA = Metropolitan Museum of Modern Art, New York
MNMB = Musée National Message Biblique Marc Chagall, Nice
RMSP = Russian Museum, St. Petersburg,

ANONYMOUS
1. *Elijah's Fiery Ascension*, 16th century, tempera on panel, 100 x 64 cm. (TGM) 31 W; **2.** *Elijah's Fiery Ascension*, 16th century, tempera on panel, 122 x 104 cm. (TGM) 31 W; **3.** *Madonna and Child*, 13th century, tempera on panel, 140 x 92 cm. (TGM) 12 W; **4.** *The Transfiguration of Christ*, 1403, tempera on panel, 184 x 134 cm. (TGM) 12 D
ALTMAN, NATAN ISAEVICH
5. *Cow and Ox*, 1914, color pencils on paper, 21.5 x 21.6 cm. (RMSP) 17 W
BACON, FRANCIS
6. *Painting*, 1946, oil and pastel on linen, 197.8 x 132.1 cm. (MOMA) 57 W
BAKST, LÉON
7. Design for the *Great Eunuch*, 1910, gouache and watercolor on paper (Strasbourg, Musée des Beaux Arts) 9 W; **8.** Design for the costume of *Narcissus*, 1911, pencil, gouache, bronze colors on paper (London, The Fine Arts Society) 19 W; **9.** *Portrait of Sergei Diaghilev*, 1906 (RMSP) 18 W; **10.** Stage design for the ballet *Schéhérazade*, 1910, gouache and watercolor on paper (Paris, Musée des Arts Décoratifs) 19 W
BISHOP, ISABEL
11. *Virgil and Dante in Union Square*, 1932, oil on canvas, 68.5 x 132 cm. (Wilmington, Delaware Art Museum) 52 W
BOCCIONI, UMBERTO
12. *The City Rises*, 1910, oil on canvas, 199.3 x 301 cm. (MOMA, Mrs Simon Guggenheim Fund) 20 W
BRANCUSI, CONSTANTIN
13. *Endless Column*, 1937, steel, height 29.35 m. (Tirgu Jiu, public gardens) 36 W
BRAQUE, GEORGES
14. *The Clarinet*, 1912, oil on canvas, 91.4 x 64.5 cm. (PGC) 21 W
CASORATI, FELICE
15. *Silvana Cenni*, 1922, oil on canvas, 205 x 105 cm. (Turin, private collection) 33 W
CÉZANNE, PAUL
16. *Portrait of Ambroise Vollard*, 1899, oil on canvas, 101 x 82 cm. (Paris, Musée du Petit Palais) 42 D
CHAGALL, MARC
17. *Abraham and the Three Angels*, 1956-58, oil on canvas, 190 x 292 cm. (MNMB) 61 W; **18.** *Abraham's Sacrifice*, 1931-39, etching, 28 x 22 cm. (MNMB) 45 W; **19.** *The Acrobat*, 1930, oil on canvas, 65 x 52 cm. (MNAM) 42 W; **20.** *Around Her*, 1945, oil on canvas, 131 x 109.5 cm. (MNAM) 54 W, D, 55 D; **21.** *The Beautiful Circus Rider*, 1930 (London, Christie's) 42 W; **22.** *Bella in Mourillon*, 1926, oil on canvas, 46 x 65 cm.(Paris, Ida Chagall Archives) 40 W; **23.** *Bella with a White Collar*, 1917, oil on canvas, 149 x 72 cm. (MNAM) 33 W; **24.** Ceiling of the Paris Opera, 1962-64, fresco (Paris, L'Opéra National) 58 W; **25.** *The Cemetery*, 1917, oil on canvas, 69.3 x 100 cm. (MNAM) 34 W; **26.** *Chichikov at Pliushkin's*, 1924-25, etching, 27.6 x 21.1 cm. (TGM) 43 W; **27.** *The Creation of Man*, 1956-58, oil on canvas, 300 x 250 cm. (MNMB) 61 W; **28.** *The Crow and the Fox*, etching, 28 x 23 cm. (MNAM) 43 W; **29.** *Dance*, 1920, tempera and kaolin on canvas, 214 x 108.5 cm. (TGM) 39 W; **30.** *The Donkey and the Dog*, etching, 28 x 23 cm. (MNAM) 43 W; **31.** *The Donkey Loaded with Sponges and the Donkey Loaded with Salt*, etching, 28 x 23 cm. (MNAM) 43 W; **32.** *Double Portrait with Wineglass*, 1917-18, oil on canvas, 233 x 136 cm. (MNAM) 32 W; **33.** *Drama*, 1920, tempera and kaolin on canvas, 212 x 107.2 cm. (TGM) 39 W; **34.** *The Flayed Ox*, 1947, oil on canvas, 100 x 81 cm. (Paris, Ida Chagall Archives) 56 W, D; **35.** *The Flowers*, 1951, ceramic plaque, 31.8 x 24.8 cm. (Paris, private collection) 59 W; **35.** *God Creates Man and Gives Him Life*, 1931-39, etching, 28 x 22 cm. (MNMB) 44 W; **37.** *God Reveals Himself to Moses*, 1931-39, etching, 28 x 22 cm. (MNMB) 44 W; **38.** *Golgotha*, 1912, oil on canvas, 174 x 191 cm. (MOMA) 25 W, 51 D; **39.** *The Green Violinist*, 1923, oil on canvas, 198 x 108.6 cm. (New York, The Solomon R. Guggenheim Museum) 23 W, D; **40.** *Homage to Apollinaire*, 1911-12, oil on canvas, 209 x 198 cm. (Eindhoven, Stedelijk Van Abbemuseum) 15 W; **41.** *I and the Village*, 1911-12, oil on canvas, 191.2 x 150.5 cm. (MOMA) 6 W; **42** *Ida at the Window*, 1924, oil on canvas, 105 x 75 cm. (Amsterdam, Stedelijk Museum) 41 W; **43.** *In My Home*, 1943, gouache on paper, 51 x 58 cm. (Turin, Modern Art Gallery) 52 W; **44.** *Introduction to the Jewish Theater*, 1920, tempera and kaolin on canvas, 284 x 787 cm. (TGM) 38-39 W, 17 D; **45.** *Jacob Struggling with the Angel*, 1931-39, etching, 28 x 22 cm. (MNMB) 45 W; **46.** *Joseph Stripped by His Brothers*, 1931-39, etching, 28 x 22 cm. (MNMB) 44 D, 45 W; **47.** *The Laughing Man and the Fish*, etching, 28 x 23 cm. (MNAM) 43 W; **48.** *Lilies of the Valley*, 1916, oil on cardboard, 40.8 x 32.1 cm. (TGM) 40 W; **49.** *Literature*, 1920, tempera and kaolin on canvas, 216 x 81.3 cm. (TGM) 39 W; **50.** *Lot and His Daughters*, 1931-39, etching, 28 x 22 cm. (MNMB) 45 W; **51.** *The Lovers at the Eiffel Tower*, 1938-39, oil on canvas, 150 x 136.5 cm. (MNAM) 46 W, D; **52.** *Lovers in the Lilacs*, 1930, oil on canvas, 128 x 87 cm. (New York, private collection) 40 W; **53.** *A Midsummer Night's Dream*, 1939, oil on canvas, 117 x 88.5 cm. (Grenoble, Musée de Peinture et de Sculpture) 48 W; **54.** *The Mirror*, 1915, oil on cardboard, 100 x 81 cm. (RMSP) 26 W; **55.** *Moses Causes Darkness to Fall Upon Egypt*, 1931-39, etching, 28 x 22 cm. (MNMB) 45 W; **56.** *Moses Receiving the Tablets of the Law*, 1956-58, oil on canvas, 238 x 234 cm. (MNMB) 60 W; **57.** *The Mother in Front of the Oven*, 1914, oil on cardboard on canvas, 63 x 47.5 cm. (Paris, Ida Chagall Archives) 27 W; **58.** *Music*, 1920, tempera and kaolin on canvas, 213 x 104 cm. (TGM) 39 W; **59.** *My Fiancée Wearing Black Gloves*, 1909, oil on canvas, 88 x 65 cm. (Basel, Oeffentliche Kunstsammlung Basel, Kunstmuseum) 8 W; **60.** *My Uncle's Store in Lyozno*, 1914, tempera, oil, and color pencil on paper, 37.1 x 49 cm. (TGM) 26 W; **61.** *Noah Releases the Dove*, 1931-39, etching, 28 x 22 cm. (MNMB) 45 W; **62.** *Over the Town*, 1914-18 (TGM) 10 D, 33 W; **63.** *Over Vitebsk*, 1915-20, oil on canvas, 67 x 92.7 cm. (MOMA) 30 W, D; **64.** Study for *Over Vitebsk*, 1914, oil on cardboard, 19.5 x 25 cm. (St. Petersburg, Nadezhda Simina Collection) 30 W; **65.** *Paris from the Window*, 1913, oil on canvas, 135.8 x 141.4 cm. (New York, The Solomon R. Guggenheim Museum) 47 W, D; **66.** *Peasant Life*, 1917-19, oil on cardboard, 21 x 21.5 cm. (Private collection) 36 W; **67.** *The Pink House* (or *The Street*), 1922, tempera with gouache on cardboard, 52 x 66 cm. (Paris, Musée d'Art Moderne de la Ville) 27 W; **68.** *Pliushkin's Room*, 1924-25, etching, 27.7 x 21.6 cm. (TGM) 43 W; **69.** *The Poet Reclining*, 1915, oil on cardboard, 77.2 x 77.5 cm. (London, The Tate Gallery) 40 W; **70.** *Pregnant Woman*, 1913, oil on canvas, 194 x 115 cm. (Amsterdam, Stedelijk Museum) 27 W; **71.** *The Promenade*, 1917-18, oil on canvas, 170 x 163.5 cm. (RMSP) 10 D, 32 W; **72.** *The Rabbi of Vitebsk*, 1914, oil on canvas, 104 x 84 cm. (Venice, Ca' Pesaro Museum of Modern Art) 7 W; **73.** *The Rainbow, a Sign of the Alliance Between God and Men*, 1952, etching, 28 x 22 cm. (MNMB) 44 W; **74.** *The Red Horse*, 1938-44, oil on canvas, 114 x 103 cm. (Nantes, Musée des Beaux-Arts) 17 W; **75.** *The Red Jew*, 1914-15, oil on cardboard, 100 x 80.5 cm. (RMSP) 26 W; **76.** *Red Roofs*, 1953-54, oil on paper on canvas, 250 x 213 cm. (Paris, private collection) 47 D; **77.** *The Refugees*, 1914, ink drawing on paper, 22.3 x 17.2 cm. (TGM) 34 W; **78.** Study for *The Revolution*, 1937, charcoal, pastel, and oil on canvas, 33.5 x 50.7 cm. (MNAM) 28 W, D; **79.** *Self-Portrait*, 1907, pencil and watercolor on paper, 20.5 x 16.5 cm. (MNAM) 10 W; **80.** *Self-Portrait*, 1908, oil on canvas, 30 x 24.5 cm. (Grenoble, Musée de Peinture et de Sculpture) 10 W; **81.** *Self-Portrait*, 1959-68, oil on canvas, 61.5 x 51 cm. (Florence, Uffizi) 11 W, 46 D; **82.** *Self-Portrait in Green*, 1914, oil on cardboard on canvas, 70 x 50 cm. (MNAM) 11 W; **83.** *Self-Portrait with Head Upside-down*, pencil and ink on paper, 29.1 x 22.2 cm. (TGM) 10 W; **84.** *Self-Portrait with Seven Fingers*, 1912-13, oil on canvas, 128 x 107 cm. (Amsterdam, Stedelijk Museum) 15 W, 16 D, 46 D; **85.** *Solitude*, 1933, oil on canvas, 102 x 169 cm. (Tel Aviv, Art Museum) 17 W; **86.** *The Soul of the City*, 1945, oil on canvas, 107 x 82 cm. (MNAM) 54 W, 55 D; **87.** Stained glass window (All Saints Church, Tudeley, England) 59 W; **88.** *The Synagogue*, 1917, tempera on paper, 40 x 35 cm. (Private collection) 27 W; **89.** *To Russia, Asses, and Others*, 1911-12, oil on canvas, 156 x 122 cm. (MNAM) 16 W, D; **90.** *View from the Window in Vitebsk*, 1908, oil on canvas on cardboard, 67 x 58 cm. (St.Petersburg, Gordeyeva Collection) 6 W; **91.** *View from the Window in Vitebsk*, 1914-15, oil, tempera, and pencil on paper, 49 x 36.5 cm. (TGM) 26 W; **92.** *The Violinist*, 1912-13, oil on canvas, 188 x 158 cm. (Amsterdam, Stedelijk Museum) 22 W, D; **93.** *The Vollard Circus*, 1927, tempera on cardboard, 38.2 x 34 cm. (Paris, Musée d'Art Moderne de la Ville) 42 W; **94.** *War on the Palaces*, 1918-19, watercolor, China ink, and pencil on paper, 33.7 x 23.2 cm. (TGM) 28 W; **95.** *The Wedding*, 1909, oil on canvas (Zurich, Emil G. Bührle Foundation) 23 W; **96.** *The Wedding Candles*, 1945, oil on canvas, 123 x 120 cm. (Paris, private collection) 23 D, 55 W, D; **97.** *The White Crucifixion*, 1938, oil on canvas, 155 x 140 cm. (Chicago, The Art Institute) 50 W, D, 51 D; **98.** *Window*, 1924, oil on canvas, 100.5 x 73.5 cm. (Zurich, Kunsthaus) 41 W; **99.** *Window in Zaolcha*, 1915, tempera and oil on cardboard, 100 x 80.5 cm. (TGM) 41 W; **100.** *The Wolf, the Goat, and the Kid*, etching, 28 x 23 cm. (MNAM) 43 W; **101.** *The Wounded Soldier*, 1914, oil on cardboard (Philadelphia, Museum of Art) 34 W
DALI, SALVADOR
102. *Premonition of the Civil War or Soft Construction with Boiled Beans*, 1936, oil on canvas, 100 x 99 cm. (Philadelphia, Museum of Art) 48 W
DE CHIRICO, GIORGIO
103. *The Enigma of the Hour*, 1911, oil on canvas (Milan, Mattioli private collection) 21 W; **104.** *Self-portrait*, 1924, oil on canvas, 38.5 x 51 cm. (Toledo, The Toledo Museum of Art) 33 W
DE KOONING, WILLEM
105. *Composition*, 1958, oil on paper mounted on masonite mounted on wood, 58.5 x 74 cm. (PGC) 52 W
DELAUNAY, ROBERT
106. *The City*, 1910, oil on canvas, 26.7 x 40.6 cm. (MNAM) 20 W
DELVAUX, PAUL
107. *Aurora*, 1937, oil on canvas, 120 x 150.5 cm. (PGC) 48 W
DIX, OTTO
108. *War*, 1914, oil on cardboard, 98.5 x 69.5 cm. (Düsseldorf, Kunstmuseum) 24 D
DOBUZHINSKY, MSTISLAV
109. *The Hairdresser's Shop Window*, 1906, watercolor on paper, 28.2 x 29 cm. (TGM) 9 W
DUCHAMP, MARCEL
110. *Nude Descending a Staircase no. 1*, 1911, oil on canvas (Philadelphia, Museum of Art) 21 W
ERNST, MAX
111. *The Robing of the Bride*, 1938-40, oil on canvas, 129.6 x 96.3 cm. (PGC) 49 W
GIOTTO
112. *The Ecstasy of St. Francis*, fresco, 1290-95, 270 x 230 cm. (Upper Church of St. Francis, Assisi) 31 W; **113.** *The Vision of the Fiery Chariot*, fresco, 1290-95, 270 x 230 cm.(Upper Church of St. Francis, Assisi) 31 W
GOLOVIN, ALEXANDER
114. Sketch for a backdrop for *Boris Godunov*, 1907, cardboard, watercolor, and gouache, 72 x 85 cm. (Moscow, Bakhrushin State Central Theatrical Museum) 19 W
GONCHAROVA, NATALIA
115. *The Bleaching of the Canvas*, 1908, oil on canvas (RMSP) 12 W
GORKY, ARSHILE
116. *Untitled*, 1944, oil on canvas, 167 x 178.2 cm. (PGC) 52 W
GRIS, JUAN
117. *The Three Cards*, 1913, oil on canvas, 45.5 x 46 cm. (Berne, Kunstmuseum, Rupf Foundation) 21 W
GROSZ, GEORGE
118. *Metropolis*, 1916-17, oil on canvas, 100 x 102 cm. (Lugano, Thyssen-Bornemisza Collection); **119.** *The Street*, 1915, oil on cardboard, 45.5 x 35.5 cm. (Stuttgart, Staatsgalerie) 24 W
HOPPER, EDWARD
120. *Night Hawks*, 1942, oil on canvas, 76.2 x 144 cm. (Chicago, The Art Institute) 53 W
KANDINSKY, WASSILY
121. *First Abstract Watercolor*, 1910, watercolor, 50 x 65 cm. (Paris, Nina Kandinsky's private collection) 36 W; **122.** *A Red Church*, 1908, oil on panel, 28 x 19.2 cm. (RMSP) 13 W
KIRCHNER, ERNST LUDWIG
123. *Five Women on the Street*, 1913, oil on canvas, 120.5 x 91 cm. (Cologne, Museum Ludwig) 25 W
KUPKA, FRANTISEK
124. *Verticals*, 1911-12, oil on canvas, 58 x 72 cm. (MNAM) 20 D
KUSTODIEV, BORIS
125. *Carnival*, 1916, oil on canvas (RMSP) 13 W
LÉGER, FERNAND
126. *Woman in Blue*, 1912, oil on canvas, 194 x 130 cm. (Basel, Kunstmuseum) 21 W
LISSITSKY, EL
127. *Hit the Whites with the Red Wedge*, 1919, poster 35 W
MAFAI, MARIO
128. *Quartered Ox*, oil on canvas, 113 x 93.5 cm. (Milan, Pinacoteca di Brera) 57 W
MAGRITTE, RENÉ
129. *The Treason of Images*, 1928-29, oil on canvas, 58.5 x 94 cm. (Los Angeles, County Museum of Art) 49 W; **130.** *The Voice of Air*, 1931, oil on canvas, 72.7 x 54.2 cm. (PGC) 49 W
MALEVICH, KAZIMIR SEVERINOVICH
131. *Black Circle*, c.1923, oil on canvas, 105 x 105 cm. (RMSP) 37 W; **132.** *Black Cross*, c.1923, oil on canvas, 106 x 106 cm. (RMSP) 37 W; **133.** *Black Square*, 1923, oil on canvas, 106 x 106 cm. (RMSP) 37 W; **134.** *Suprematism no. 58 with Yellow and Black*, 1916 (RMSP) 35 W
MARC, FRANZ
135. *The Red Roe Deer*, 1912, oil on canvas, 170 x 100 cm. (Munich, Staatsgalerie Moderner Kunst) 25 W
MASSON, ANDRÉ
136. Ceiling of the Odéon National Theater, 1965, fresco (Paris, Théâtre National de l'Odéon) 59 W
MATISSE, HENRI
137. *Interior with Eggplants*, 1911, tempera on canvas, 212 x 246 cm. (Grenoble, Musée de Peinture et de Sculpture) 21 W; **138.** *Luxury II*, 1907, 209.5 x 139 cm. (Copenhagen, Statens Museum for Kunst) 20 W
MODIGLIANI, AMEDEO
139. *Head*, 1911-12, stone sculpture, 63.5 x 12.5 x 35 cm. (London, The Trustees of the Tate Gallery) 21 W
MONDRIAN, PIETER CORNELIS
140. *Blossoming Apple Tree*, c.1912, oil on canvas, 78 x 106 cm. (The Hague, Gemeentemuseum) 37 W; **141.** *Blue Tree*, 1909-10, oil on anvas, 75.5 x 99.5 cm. (The Hague, Gemeentemuseum) 37 W; **142.** *Gray Tree*, 1912, oil on canvas, 78.5 x 107.5 cm. (The Hague, Gemeentemuseum) 37 W; **143.** *Red Tree*, 1908, oil on canvas, 70 x 99 cm. (The Hague, Gemeentemuseum) 37 W
MONET, CLAUDE
144. *Water Lilies*, 1908, oil on canvas (Paris, Musée d'Orsay) 40 D
PETROV-VODKIN, KUZMA
145. *Red Horse Bathing*, 1912, oil on canvas, 180 x 186 cm. (TGM) 17 W
PICASSO, PABLO
146. *Les Demoiselles d'Avignon*, 1907, oil on canvas, 243.9 x 233.7 cm. (MOMA) 20 W; **147.** *The Poet*, 1911, oil on canvas, 131.2 x 89.5 cm. (PGC) 21 W; **148.** *The Race*, 1922, tempera on plywood, 32.5 x 41.1 cm. (Paris, Picasso Museum) 32 W
POLLOCK, JACKSON
149. *Moon-Woman*, 1942, oil on canvas, 137 x 110 cm. (PGC) 53 W
PORDENONE, GIOVANNI ANTONIO
150. *Crucifixion*, 1520, fresco, 920 x 1200 cm. (Cremona Cathedral) 51 W
RASTRELLI, BARTOLOMEO CARLO
151. Bust of Peter the Great, 1723-29, bronze, 102 x 90 x 40 cm. (St. Petersburg, Hermitage Museum) 8 W
REMBRANDT, VAN RIJN
152. *The Quartered Ox*, 1655, oil on canvas, 94 x 67 cm. (Paris, Louvre) 57 W
SEVERINI, GINO
153. *North-South*, 1912, oil on canvas, 49 x 64 cm. (Milan, Pinacoteca di Brera)
SIMONE MARTINI
154. *The Blessed Agostino Novello and His Four Miracles*, 1325-28, tempera on panel, 65 x 67 cm. (Siena, Pinacoteca Nazionale) 31 W
SOUTINE, CHAIM
155. *Skinned Ox*, 1925, oil on canvas, 202 x 114 cm. (Grenoble, Musée de Peinture et de Sculpture) 57 W
TATLIN, VLADIMIR
156. Model for a monument to the Third International, 1919-20, metal and painted wood reconstruction, height 3 m., diameter 1.56 m. (Stockholm, Moderna Museet) 28 W
TITIAN
157. *Portrait of a Man*, c.1515, oil on canvas, 81.2 x 66.3 cm. (London, National Gallery) 11 W, D
UTRILLO, MAURICE
158. *View of Montmartre*, c.1910., oil on canvas , 50 x 61 cm. (MNAM) 15 W
VRUBEL, MIKHAIL
159. *Six-Winged Seraph*, 1904, oil on canvas (RMSP) 12 W
WILLINK, CAREL A.
160. *Wilma*, 1933, oil on canvas, 153 x 107 cm. (The Hague, Gemeente-museum) 33 W
WOOD, GRANT
161. *American Gothic*, 1930, oil on canvas (Chicago, The Art Institute) 33 W
YUON, KONSTANTIN
162. *Red Planet*, 1921 (TGM) 28 W

♦ CREDITS

The original and previously unpublished illustrations in this book were created at the request of, and by, DoGi s.r.l., who holds the copyright.
ILLUSTRATIONS: Manuela Cappon (12-13); Louis R. Galante (4-5; 28-29; 60-61); Claudia Saraceni (6-7; 8-9; 14-15; 18-19; 24-25; 34-35; 48-49; 52-53)
COVER: Claudia Saraceni

REPRODUCTIONS OF ARTISTS' WORKS:
ALINARI/GIRAUDON: 9, 35, 54, 75, 92, 134; ALINARI/LAUROS/GIRAUDON: 7, 15, 98, 106; AMSTERDAM, STEDELIJK MUSEUM: 42, 84; ARTEPHOT/M. BABEY: 121; ARTEPHOT/ROLAND: 76, 78, 96; ARTOTHEK: 70, 90, 154, 162; BASEL, OEFFENTLICHE KUNSTSAMMLUNG: 59, 126; BERNE, KUNSTMUSEUM, HERMAN U. MARGRIT RUPF-STIFTUNG: 117; CHICAGO, THE ART INSTITUTE: 97, 120, 161; COLOGNE, MUSEUM LUDWIG/RHEINISCHES BILDARCHIV: 123; COPENHAGEN, STATENS MUSEUM FOR KUNST, SOELVGADE/HANS PETERSEN: 138; DELAWARE ART MUSEUM: 11; DoGi ARCHIVES (QUATTRONE): 112, 113; DoGi ARCHIVES: 3, 14, 52, 66, 102, 127, 144, 145, 146, 147, 148,; EINDHOVEN, STEDELIJK VAN ABBESMUSEUM: 40; FLORENCE, SCALA: 41, 53, 103, 125, 145, 150, 153, 155; GRENOBLE, MUSEE DE GRENOBLE: 80, 137; IDA CHAGALL ARCHIVES: 22, 34, 57; LONDON, THE TATE GALLERY: 69; LONDON, TRUSTEES OF THE NATIONAL GALLERY: 157; MILAN, PINACOTECA DI BRERA/GIANFARINI: 128; MOSCOW, BAKHRUSHIN STATE CENTRAL THEATRICAL MUSEUM: 114; MOSCOW, TRETYAKOV GALLERY: 1, 2, 3, 4, 26, 29, 33, 44, 48, 49, 58, 60, 62, 68, 77, 83, 91, 94, 99, 109; NEW YORK, METROPOLITAN MUSEUM OF MODERN ART: 6, 12, 38, 63; NEW YORK, SOLOMON R. GUGGENHEIM FOUNDATION: 39, 65; NICE, MUSEE NATIONAL MESSAGE BIBLIQUE MARC CHAGALL: 18, 36, 37, 45, 46, 50, 55, 61, 73; PARIS, MUSEE NATIONAL D'ART MODERNE – CENTRE POMPIDOU/PHOTO PHILIPPE MIGEAT: 31, 47, 89, 100; PARIS, MUSEE NATIONAL D'ART MODERNE – CENTRE POMPIDOU: 19, 20, 23, 25, 28, 30, 32, 51, 79, 82, 86, 124; PHILADELPHIA, PHILADELPHIA MUSEUM OF ART: 101; PHOTO VILLE DE NANTES – MUSEE DES BEAUX ARTS: 74; PHOTOTHEQUE DES MUSEES DE LA VILLE DE PARIS: 67, 93; QUATTRONE: 81; RMN/GERARD BLOT: 17, 27, 56, 152; ST. PETERSBURG, RUSSIAN MUSEUM: 5, 64, 115, 122, 131, 132, 133; STOCKHOLM, STATENS KONSMUSEER: 156; STUTTGART, STAATSGALERIE: 119; THE BRIDGEMAN ART LIBRARY: 8, 10, 16, 21, 24, 71, 72, 85, 87, 88, 103, 108, 116, 118, 124, 129, 135, 139, 142, 143, 149, 151, 158, 159; THE HAGUE, GEMEENTEMUSEUM BELDRECHT AMSTELVEEN: 140, 141, 160; TOLEDO, THE TOLEDO MUSEUM OF ART: 104; TURIN, GALLERIA D'ARTE MODERNA/FOTO GONELLA: 43; VENICE, PEGGY GUGGENHEIM COLLECTION: 105, 107, 130; ZURICH, EMIL G. BUHRLE FOUNDATION: 95

COVER (clockwise from top left) 92, 19, 65, 32, 27, 24, 71, 146, 85, 62, 23, 53, 84, 71, 75, 51, 88, 89, 27, 162, 82, 20
DOCUMENTS: (Abbreviations: b. bottom; c. center; l. left; r. right; t. top.)
IDA CHAGALL ARCHIVES: 6 tl; ARCHIVES PHOTOS FRANCE: 48 tl, 59 tr; ARCHIVES PHOTOS FRANCE/MICHEL SIMA: 14 tl; ARCHIVIO DoGi: 7 tr; 13 tr, br; 18 tl; 36 tl, br; 38 tl; 40 tl; ODEON – THEATRE DE L'EUROPE: 59 cr
The reproduction of the works of C. Brancusi, G. Braque, F. Casorati, M. Chagall, G. De Chirico, W. de Kooning, O. Dix, M. Duchamp, M. Ernst, A. Gorky, G. Grosz, W. Kandinsky, F. Kupka, F. Léger, E. Lissitzky, R. Magritte, A. Masson, P. Picasso, J. Pollock, G. Severini has been authorised by SIAE (Italian Association of Authors and Publishers). @ by SIAE, 1997. The works of H. Matisse, @ by succ. Matisse; the works of S. Dali, @ Fundació Gala – Salvador Dali. For their respective works, @ by: N.I. Altman, F. Bacon, I. Bishop, R. Delaunay, P. Delvaux, M. Dobuzhinsky, E. Hopper, E.L. Kirchner, J. Konstantin, N. Mafai, P.C. Mondrian, K. Petrov-Vodkin, C. Soutine, W. Tatlin, M. Utrillo, C.A. Willink.

DoGi s.r.l. has made every effort to trace other possible copyright holders. If any omissions or errors have been made, this will be corrected at reprint.